LYRICAL INTERFERENCE
ESSAYS ON POETICS

Norman Finkelstein

SPUYTEN DUYVIL

New York City

ISBN 0-9720662-2-5

Spuyten Duyvil, 1-800-886-5304; http://spuytenduyvil.net

The essays in this volume originally appeared in the following publications. My
thanks to the editors for their interest in my work:
"Pressing for the End": *Ironwood* 14.1 (Spring 1986).
"Project and Utterance": *Denver Quarterly* 23.3/4 (Winter/Spring 1989).
"Statement and Commentary": *Denver Quarterly* 30.4 (Spring 1996).
"Two Problems in Recent American Poetry": Part I (as "The Problem of the Self in
Recent American Poetry") in *Poetics Journal* 9 (June 1991); Part II (as "Language
Poetry and the Problem of the Avant-Garde") in *Talisman* 9 (Fall 1992).
"The Academy, the Avant-Garde, and the Poet-Critic: Historical Observations,
Hermeneutical Speculations": previously unpublished.
"The Serial Poem, Dictation, and the Status of the Lyric": *The Recovery of the Public
World: Essays on Poetics in Honour of Robin Blaser*, ed. Charles Watts & Edward
Byrne, Talonbooks, 1999.
"'Lyrical Interference' in *The New American Poetry*": previously unpublished.
"Bronk, Duncan, and the Far Border of Poetry": *Sagetrieb* 12.3 (Winter 1993).
"Some Reflections on Poetic Inspiration": *Denver Quarterly* 28.3 (Winter 1994).
"Poetry and Emotion": *Encyclopedia of Human Emotions*, ed. David Levinson, James
J. Ponzetti, Jr, & Peter F. Jorgensen, Macmillan Reference USA, 1999.

Library of Congress Cataloging-in-Publication Data

Finkelstein, Norman, 1954-
Lyrical interference : essays on poetics / Norman Finkelstein.
p. cm.
ISBN 0-9720662-2-5
1. American poetry--20th century--History and criticism. 2.
Poetics--History--20th century. I. Title.
PS323.5 .F56 2003
811'.509--dc21   2003014238

Contents

INTRODUCTION

Laureates and eponymous lines of high-end greeting cards aside, American poetry is not quite yet a Decorative Art. Whitman's "Nature without check with original energy" gives and takes refreshment without the sanction of national, state or metropolitan authorities and without pause for the consolatory or confessional Muse. Mullein and poke-weed outspeed the laurel. Friendship is a credential no colleges confer. American poetry is green and vivid, even wild and mischievous sometimes, among its friends. And right now it has no better friend than the poet and scholar-of-many-single-pages Norman Finkelstein, whose best essays you are about to read.

I first met Norman in a D.H. Lawrence seminar in the autumn of 1973. We were both then Juniors, English majors in a happy pantisocracy called Harpur College. Almost immediately, he became the first, best teacher of poetry I have ever had. I delight to remember the pair of us cross-legged on a Murphy bed (I swear this is true; it *was* a Murphy bed) in Johnson City, New York. I recited pages from *Lord Weary's Castle* to him. And Norman, thank God, replied with Charles Olson's "The Distances." I can still see him: Olson's skinny blue book in his right hand, a thick clutch of his own brown hair in the left. I'd been intoning a cluttered metaphysics, making the small dark room smaller and darker. But when it was Norman's turn to recite, light and air and an open path for them to travel cosmologized the apartment. If I had had the intelligence to honor Robert Creeley then as I honor and love him now, surely a certain classic poem would have sprung into my mind.

As I sd to my
friend, because I am
always talking,—John, I

sd, which was not his
name, the darkness sur-
rounds us, what

can we do against
it, or else, shall we &
why not, buy a goddamn big car,

drive, he sd, for
christ's sake, look
out where yr going.
("I Know a Man")

In 1973, poetry was a darkness surrounding me, and I took too-strange pleasure in saying so. And then I began to hear what Norman Finkelstein had to say and to share. There were places, wide vatic places, to go, and there were vehicles and drivers and lights along the way. (Kind of wonderful that Norman's first car was a Nova.) The vehicles were projective and objectivist, supercharged for series and seriality and even epic sometimes: American-made chariots of fire. The information is all here in these essays. The names are a company Norman has envisioned and loved and so joined. Here is the road work and engineering of an indecorous sagacity and sublime. Nothing could be more serious nor more full of mirth.

The wild is always unprecedented, but never inconsistent. This is the knowledge that makes American scholarship American. Norman Finkelstein offers unprecedented insights here whose facts consist of one Soul purpose: Friendship. Here the imagination of poetry is Friendship *on* the line. And driving that line are energies of the inevitable (if we are to live, Friendship is inevitable): motions outward; an outstretched hand; a goddamn big car bought and paid for lovingly.

These energies speak simply, and doing so, they accomplish new simplicities which Finkelstein boldly proposes as the most radical virtues of poetic art. Read and see. Read and go. After three decades of such virtue, Norman Finkelstein has more than earned the right to quote and to own this beautiful line from William Bronk's "The Tell":

You are my friend. The world is beautiful.

Reader, take this book to heart. And be cheerful, because it is true.

Donald Revell
Las Vegas, Nevada
December 2002

PREFACE

The essays in this volume were written over a span of about fifteen years, from 1985 to 2000. They reflect my thinking about poetics during that period, when I also wrote *The Utopian Moment in Contemporary American Poetry*, *The Ritual of New Creation*, *Not One of Them In Place*, and my first two books of poetry, *Restless Messengers* and *Track* (Volume I). Poetry or the criticism of poetry obviously has occupied nearly all my time as a writer, and readers may reasonably ask if these pieces really add to what I've already had to offer—a question which, at first, I asked myself as well. What I discovered in gathering these essays, however, is a surprisingly coherent set of themes and concerns, shaped partly by external developments in American poetry during those years, and partly by what I can only call my inner poetic life. In fact, I am now tempted to regard this book as central to my work, for it is in these pieces, however disparate and occasional their original production, that I was able to think through the issues and establish the positions which inform all my other projects. These include the relationship of poetic rhetorics to aesthetic ideologies (especially in experimental poetry); the role of influence in the determination of literary value; the status of the canon, the academy, and the avant-garde in a changing cultural climate; and the particular psychic forces that shape poetic utterance.

In planning this selection, I decided not to include the essays and reviews I have written on individual poets; the reappearance of those pieces will have to wait for another occasion. But readers of my other works will certainly recognize in these pages those figures in modern poetry who have become my personal touchstones. Part of the pleasure in writing some of these essays came from my engagements, fugitive as they might be, with, say, Shakespeare, Keats, or Dickinson, in addition to my longstanding interest in Pound, Duncan, or Bronk. What this means, I suppose, is that in these essays, I am writing much more as a poet than an academic critic, though some of them arose out of academic circumstances such as lectures, conference papers, and reference articles. In retrospect, this too has been a source of pleasure, though perhaps a more ironic one, given that the institutional status and social functions of poetry are often the actual subjects of the essays.

But not always. I have frequently noted that I write about the poetry I enjoy reading in order to explain to myself why I write my own. As Jack Spicer puts it in *Admonitions*, "Muses do exist, but now I know that they are not afraid to dirty their hands with explication—that they are patient with truth and commentary as long as it doesn't get into the poem, that they whisper (if you let yourself really hear them), 'Talk all you want, baby, but *then* let's go to bed.'" I have always tried to follow those ladies' advice.

This is one of a number of reasons why I've chosen to call this book *Lyrical Interference*. The title comes from Charles Olson's "Projective Verse," in which he speaks of "getting rid of the lyrical interference of the individual as ego, of the 'subject' and his soul," replacing this interference with "objectism," Olson's version of objectivism. As much as I value the objectivist project in general, I have always found that particular move rather dubious, and taken together, these essays explain why. In other words, these essays are my lyrical interference in the poetic affairs of the times, especially on behalf of the subject and his soul, which are never as easily jettisoned as some of my elders and contemporaries have believed. In Spicer's terms, this lyrical interference is the talk to which his muses refer, or, to shift to a less erotic metaphor, the noise out of which emerges the enigmatic poetry of dictation coming from the radio in Cocteau's *Orphée*. Spicer tries to keep that interference out of his poetry, but never fully succeeds. No poet can, because the counter-truth, which Harold Bloom has codified, is that all poetry is always already a commentary. How that commentary is articulated—*the shape of its utterance*—is what we value in poetics or in poetry.

Cincinnati, Ohio   July, 2002

PRESSING FOR THE END

for Ross Feld

I

It has often been noted that as a given century nears its close, society grows more apocalyptic in its outlook. Fortune tellers, cults and pseudo-sciences of all sorts abound; St. John the Divine and Nostradamus vie with nuclear weapons and UFOs to seize the popular imagination; Yeats' rough beast is always reborn. And simply because our century actually possesses the material means to bring about at least one version of the apocalypse, it remains debatable whether such knowledge imposes itself on the imagination in any more forceful ways than did the End of Days in previous centuries: for art, the vision of nuclear winter described in the latest scientific bulletin bears no more nor less emotional reality than that of the seven angels who assume such monumental proportions in the Book of Revelation. In terms of eschatology (at least), there is only one level of reality for art.

But for some sensibilities—and I would have to include mine—it does not require the end of a century to be charged with the imaginative potential of the End of Days. Granted, it would not take a historian to argue that any moment of the twentieth century could be deemed apocalyptic; hence the continued relevance of Walter Benjamin's final reminder that for the Jews, "every second of time was the strait gate through which the Messiah might enter." Furthermore, in thinking of Benjamin and Messianism in our time, it is worth considering the old notion in Jewish theology that the Messiah will appear only in an age of total purity or total corruption, the latter view having always resulted in the greater historical consequences. On the other hand, we also find continual warnings against "pressing for the End," that is, daring to act in the human sphere in such a way as to speed the moment of redemption—warnings that, as Gershom Scholem wryly says, "have always been most offensive to the revolutionary." Such warnings must be omnipresent in rabbinic tradition because of the equally omnipresent desire on the part of the Jews—the intellectuals and the masses alike—to transform material and spiritual exile into their opposites: to experience the ingathering that was so variously interpreted in the most esoteric texts of the Talmud and Kabbalah, as well as in the simplest mishnah or folk tale. As Scholem tells us with such strength and pathos, "The magnitude of the Messianic idea corresponds to the endless powerlessness in Jewish history during all the centuries of exile, when it was unprepared to come forward onto the plane of world history." Powerlessness generates its opposite in the dialectic of the imagination as well as that of history: as the Romantics were to learn, even as the Jews had always known, to enter into the unfolding Word, through all its commentaries, is the most empowering and most futile of acts. It is nothing more or less than the signature of a life lived in hope, and as such, it rushes headlong to make an End of itself: an act which, by its very nature, it can never fully accomplish.

It seems to me that such an intuition as this can profoundly inscribe itself in a poem, creating a palimpsest which can be read from time to time as literary and historical conditions continue to change. Thus I am concerned with the poem as the bearer of certain signs which perhaps, when adequately translated, will hint at the quietest approach of the Messianic Kingdom, a concept which, for art and history alike, is far less supernatural than ordinarily would appear. In this translated realm of reading which I propose, this looking-glass world of interpretation, the poem, which purportedly announces its significance through its existence as utterance, here must be read for its gestures towards silence. Certain poems seek relentlessly to end themselves. The poem that is almost mute, that rises out of silence, suddenly sings, and as suddenly ceases, reminds us most strongly of our struggle for linguistic plenitude, a struggle which began, as Benjamin would put it, with the Fall, "the decay of the blissful, Adamite language-mind" that was directly in touch with the boundlessly creative Word. The Fall of the language-mind, for our purposes, corresponds to the severe limitations and distortions imposed upon language by its production within history. In the fallen world, the poem's language encloses itself and always gestures to the silence that lies immediately beyond it.

The poem's significance thus resides less in its opening of itself to speech (often among the most profane of acts), but in its closing of itself to such temptation. The poem in its utterance presents itself as an act of resistance to silence, even though it is bound, finally, to yield. It is at the moment the poem falls silent, enacting its closure, that a window opens upon the Messianic world. The poem is furthest from its Beginning then, and as stillness approaches, it hovers on the brink of the altogether new. Messianism, which Scholem regards as combining elements of the restorative and the utopian, is here made manifest in the poem almost exclusively through the latter element. It is at this moment that the poem, against all injunctions, is seen as pressing for the End. Its moving back into silence is simultaneously a darting forward, just as in the Kabbalistic model, the Word withdrew into itself to commence the exteriorizing creation. As in the Beginning, so at the End. But this action, however, will be repeated time after time, in poem after poem, an even surer indication of the utopian nature of this enterprise: silence struggles within the poem to be released, silence which at once signifies loss and generation.

II

To the poem as Angelus Novus, the poem addressed to silence, I bring Louis Zukofsky's dream of the poem as the totality of perfect rest. Zukofsky's "An Objective," in which this formulation may be found, is surely one of the most hermetic texts in the annals of twentieth-century poetics, and as such, it is open to endless Talmudic interpretation and disputation. Zukofsky's notion of objectification is a synthesis of two opposing tendencies, which, in the shifting tides of his elusive prose, he labels sincerity and perfection. Sincerity is to be found in language which conforms as closely as possible "with things as they exist"; while perfection is to be found in language that is self-fulfilling, "complete appreciation." These two moments are one within the objectified poem, the rested totality. It appears to me that any such poem which brings these qualities together must also, on the theologicopolitical level with which we are here concerned, bring together the opening and closing to speech which we have already deemed to be Messianic in its hidden intent. The poem that is the totality of perfect rest is that poem which may be seen, in its relation to utterance, as pressing for the End.

We may further expound upon Zukofsky's Messianic Objectivism by considering the very phrase "perfect rest." At one point in his essay, Zukofsky loosely, almost arbitrarily, strings together sentence fragments that together constellate his idea of objectification. Here are two such clusters:

Perfect rest? Or nature as creator, existing perfect, experience perfecting activity of existence, making it—theologically, perhaps—like the Ineffable?

•　•　•

The desire for what is objectively perfect, inextricably the direction of historic and contemporary particulars—A desire to place everything—everything aptly, perfectly, belonging within, one with, a context—

In the first passage, the poem as activity of existence extends outward from nature as creator, experience perfect within itself. The poem (and we are on familiar ground here) is a second nature, to be created perfect from natural experience, which was in turn created perfect by the Ineffable. The creation of the poem is meant to be an *act* of perfection, and therefore must be a complete utterance, a movement out of the stillness of natural experience, a pure, totalizing gesture of language. In the second passage, the desire for what is objectively perfect is meant to follow out the course of history, to find a place or context for all particulars, a "belonging within," a place of rest. Here, it is not the act of utterance but the *rest* from utterance, the setting of order within historical experience, that may lead again to objective, natural stillness. Thus it can be argued that Zukofsky's "perfect rest" involves the simultaneous experiences of action and cessation, the poem's Messianic identity secured through both utterance and stillness, these metaphysical as well as formal counterparts.

What remains so disturbing about Zukofsky's formulation—

although it is just this disturbance that confirms the Messianic quality of his thought—is the tendency to see the objectified poem, the rested totality, as a refuge from history as well as an active response to it. This accounts in part for the radically heterogeneous quality of "A", a poem even more at odds with itself than *The Cantos,* its immediate precursor. And it makes Zukofsky's Marxism, like that of his friend George Oppen, deeply problematic, given the piety and reverence that mark the work of both poets, especially as they near the ends of their careers. Benjamin, in distinguishing between Messianic and historical (or profane) dynamics, again helps to illuminate this situation. As he says in the "Theologico-Political Fragment," "If one arrow points to the goal toward which the profane dynamic acts, and another marks the direction of Messianic intensity, then certainly the quest of free humanity for happiness runs counter to the Messianic direction; but just as a force can, through acting, increase another that is acting in the opposite direction, so the order of the profane assists, through being profane, the coming of the Messianic Kingdom. The profane, therefore, although not itself a category of this Kingdom, is a decisive category of its quietest approach."

"The quest of free humanity for happiness" is deeply inscribed upon Objectivist texts, but no more so than the quest for redemption, which, as Benjamin pointedly notes, "is not the goal, but the end" of history. The poem as perfect rest then is a totality indeed, for in its profane linguistic activity, it must embody these two dialectically opposed forces, in order that it might become a decisive category of the Messianic Kingdom's quietest approach.

I admit that it is just this tension or inconsistency that makes the work of the Objectivists so attractive to me, and perhaps even lends it its greatest formal strengths. For no matter how bravely these poets seek to bind their work to "the direction of historic and contemporary particulars," some invisible textual agency unbinds the words, leaving them to lapse into silence. It it as if the poem can contain only so much matter before seeking its release, its permission to constitute itself not as utterance but as stillness. As Oppen says in *Of Being Numerous:*

Clarity

In the sense *of transparence,*
I don't mean that much can be explained.

Clarity in the sense of silence.

And in a different emotional register, the Valentine poems that punctuate Zukofsky's *All* likewise verge always on silence, as if love did not dare to do anything more than sing the softest and briefest of songs before passing back into the quiet passage of the calendar's leaves:

> What I did not say the other day to you for today
> Is not unsaid because lost today with such thoughts in my head
> That make one who looks up at the time say it has gone ahead.

The thoughts of love and illumination that so drive these poets move on ahead of themselves: they hasten themselves into silence, and in their Messianic trajectory language is left behind. For language can only mark where desire has been.

III

The flight from history is a flight into personality. Perhaps this is merely the converse of Eliot's dictum that only the impersonal poet can fully engage the tradition; but it should still be noted that even those poets who seek on some level to disengage themselves from historical concerns must explore themselves while remaining under the sign of historicity. For no such flight is ever really successful; indeed, the desire to dissolve the self that inevitably results from a primarily personalistic stance is the price paid for the reluctance to come forward onto the plane of world history. The poet who demonstrates such reluctance will no doubt be unable, perhaps even unwilling, to move past the silence that will surround the poem. As he sets the poem in order, an order corresponding to his immediate emotional state, he will no doubt feel that he has laid history to rest: the poem's boundary of silence will be the boundary of the personal, the boundary of time. The poem will silence itself; the poem will end.

If this is a tendency in the work of the older Objectivists, it is a pre-condition in the work of Robert Creeley. Creeley is the foremost love poet of our time because he has recognized that Love's demands are absolute, but can never be completely articulated or fulfilled. Love cannot speak nor the lover hear clearly: if Creeley's poems astonish us with their clarity, it is a clarity designed to compensate for a psycho-historical interference that encroaches upon the poem as a state of random noise and arbitrary circumstance. This is history from the point of view of the "unsure egoist," for whom erotic self-possession, to be attained through the beloved, is an absolute that is violated over and over. Here is an early poem, "For a Friend," that presents this paradigm:

> You are one man
> coming down the street on
>
> a bicycle. And love is a certainty
> because it is sure of itself.
>
> The alphabet is letters,
> the muskrat was a childhood friend.
>
> And love is eternal,
> and pathetic equally.

Because love is eternal and pathetic equally, present in desire, absent in achievement, the result is psychic pain, as in "The Flower":

> I think I grow tensions
> like flowers
> in a wood where
> nobody goes.

Each wound is perfect,
encloses itself in a tiny
imperceptible blossom,
making pain.

Pain is a flower like that one,
like this one,
like that one,
like this one.

This has always struck me as an intolerable predicament, and the realization of its truth is a prayer to stillness, which has never been so welcomed by a poem's closure. If the self as lover—and as poet—is to survive at all, it is through sudden, often violent ritual, as in "The Warning":

For love—I would
split open your head and put
a candle in
behind the eyes.

Love is dead in us
if we forget
the virtues of an amulet
and quick surprise.

But an equally valid, perhaps even more desirable?and extreme—response is that of "Oh No":

If you wander far enough
you will come to it
and when you get there
they will give you a place to sit

for yourself only, in a nice chair,
and all your friends will be there

with smiles on their faces
and they will likewise all have places.

Of Creeley's poems that are, as he would say, dear to me (I think of "The Whip" or "The Door" or "The Rain"), none of them conveys the extreme psychic impact of this one. Sartre and Beckett, of course, have written plays about such matters, but the generic demands of lyric poetry force us to turn to different rhetorical and philosophical models to appreciate this moment. Creeley is no longer a love poet here, but his arrival at this place is intimately related to the continually blocked and delayed gratification he seeks in Love's (earthly) kingdom. An existentialist would probably see this place as a sort of hell, the proper reward for a life lived in bad faith. Oh no: Creeley has wandered far enough that these terms no longer apply. Patient, enthroned among his familiars (I think of Stevens' "imagination that sits enthroned"), with all having their places, the poet has prepared a context for himself that dissolves the self and seems to place it beyond history, trembling into silent anticipation.

How is it that Creeley, the latter-day New England Puritan, should bear what Scholem tells us is "the gnostic knowledge of the *merkabah,* the throne-world of God and its mysteries which, explosive as this knowledge in itself was, could be reported only in a whisper"? I am not certain: the paths of influence grow ever more complex. But Creeley's devotion to personal, revealed truth certainly leads him to this pass; and though, for me, "Oh No" is as extreme a poem as he writes, he seems to shuttle back and forth through love and beyond it, to this place of redemptive silence, again and again. Only through this movement or process, to be seen repeatedly in that long succession of brief poems that constitute his life-work, can Creeley play out his role of Love's servant in a personal realm of desire that never seems to rest, and still acknowledge the antithetical role of one who presses for the End. Throughout that long sequence of poems (and it should be remembered that Creeley remarks upon Zukofsky's belief that a poet writes one poem all his life), I sense the arrows of Benjamin's profane and Messianic counterforces continually in motion. Do they ever cease in their flight? Here is a more recent poem:

What to say
these days
of crashing disjunct,
whine, of separation—

Not abstract—
"God's will," not
lost in clouds this
experienced wisdom.

Hand and mind
and heart one
ground to walk on,
field to plow.

I know
a story
I can tell
and will.

It is odd to consider Creeley a storyteller, but of course he is just that—and in the poems as much as in the fiction. And as Benjamin says in his great essay, "The Storyteller," "it is granted to him to reach back to a whole lifetime (a life, incidentally, that comprises not only his own experience but no little of the experience of others; what a storyteller knows from hearsay is added to his own). His gift is the ability to relate his life; his distinction, to be able to tell his entire life. The storyteller: he is the man who could let the wick of his life be consumed completely by the gentle flame of his story." When the wick of his life is consumed by the flame of the story, both story and life (which for Creeley are one in all their moments) come to an end. Ontologically speaking, when Creeley names himself as a storyteller, he completes the task of his life: he has been telling his life/story up to the moment of its telling. And with the most sublime irony, the moment that promises a beginning of utterance is in reality a closure.

The name of the poem is "Thinking of Walter Benjamin."

IV

Jack Spicer spent his entire career attempting to counter (or escape) "the big lie of the personal." For Spicer, the personal realm of Love is not to be traversed, each step of the journey dutifully recorded until one reaches the outer marches, where one can set up camp and rest. Rather, any incursion into that territory is to be viewed as particularly dangerous to the progress of the poet, for it distracts him from his true purpose, that of radio, ghostcatcher, receiver of messages from the outside. Hence Spicer's well-known critique of Creeley in *The Heads of the Town Up to the Aether,* his ironic homage to Creeley's "driving" of the poem, since for Spicer no poem worthy of the name is directed by the poet at all. Spicer's argument for the disappearance of the lyric subject, its dissolution into language, provides, however, no resolution to his agon: dictation drove him wild, for its truths were matters of personal failure that were totally congruent with political corruption in broadly historical and narrowly literary spheres. The house that Jack built collapsed because it proved too haunted for its own good.

Spicer's poetry then presents itself to us in the form of a ruin, over which always broods silence. A Spicer poem is an utterance, of course, but an utterance in which one may "hear" a personality mutely eradicating itself, willing itself into stillness against the almost irresistible urge to go on talking. If Spicer's poems are, as he would have them, messages received by a supposedly objective medium, they are messages that contain within themselves their own willful closure. Indeed, the inner content of these messages *is* their closure; what they wish to record, paradoxically, is their disappearance. Thus they are bound to be ruins, failures (as Benjamin applied the term to Kafka's works), for how can a message inform its recipient that it has failed to be delivered? How can a poem memorialize its own unmaking? And yet, uncanny as it may seem, there are poems throughout *The Collected Books* that seem to do just that, pressing forward more to enter into silence than speech. Here is "A Book of Music":

Coming at an end, the lovers
Are exhausted like two swimmers. Where
Did it end? There is no telling. No love is
Like an ocean with the dizzy procession of the waves'
boundaries
From which two can emerge exhausted, nor long goodbye
Like death.
Coming at an end. Rather, I would say, like a length
Of coiled rope
Which does not disguise in the final twists of its lengths
Its endings.
But, you will say, we loved
And some parts of us loved
And the rest of us will remain
Two persons. Yes,
Poetry ends like a rope.

This is the title poem of one of Spicer's early series, and it is the last poem in the sequence. Formally speaking, it is appropriate that the poem should be about endings; it self-consciously brings the entire group of poems to a close with its abrupt but still anticipated final line. But it is worth noting that this poem also begins by ending—"Coming at an end"—so that the entire text appears as nothing more than a set of delaying tactics for a resolution that has already been determined in advance of the utterance. In other words, the poem wants to end before it begins; it seeks fulfillment before establishing those conditions which prepare for fulfillment, implicitly negating the worth of time experienced as anterior to the End. In the erotic terms of the poem, the moment after climax or the moment after the relationship has ended embodies the entirety of content: "No love is / Like an ocean with the dizzy procession of the waves' boundaries," since the procession is secondary to that which comes after it. Alas for Spicer: a more relentlessly aggressive soul than Creeley, his entire opus becomes not a shuttling between but a pursuit, which grows increasingly more desperate as his literary and personal isolation worsens:

The moment's rest. And the bodies entangled and yet not
                            entangled in sleeping. Could we get
Out of our skins and dance? The bedclothes
So awry that they seem like two skins.
Or all the sorts of skins that we wore, wear (the orgasm),
                         wanted to wear, or would be wearing.
                         So utterly tangled. A bad dream.
A moment's rest. The skins
All of them
Near.
I saw the ghost of myself and the ghost of yourself dancing
                                    without music.
With
Out
Skin.
A good dream. The
Moment's rest.

This is the last poem in the second section of Spicer's last series, *Book of Magazine Verse*. The hope for an ending has become momentary here, and love has become monstrous, a Laocoon of devouring entanglement from which there is no escape. Love's potential to provide a sorrowful stillness or a blissful, exhausted rest is nothing more than a good dream from which the poet must inevitably wake. To understand Spicer's urgency and despair, however, we must simultaneously comprehend his attitude towards poetry, which corresponds in the course of his overreaching pursuit, to his erotic record. Indeed, when Spicer yearned so pathetically for the moment's rest, he had already come to what is, for a poet, a far more drastic point:

       This ocean, humiliating in its disguises
       Tougher than anything.
       No one listens to poetry. The ocean
       Does not mean to be listened to. A drop
       Or crash of water. It means

Nothing.
It
Is bread and butter
Pepper and salt. The death
That young men hope for. Aimlessly
It pounds the shore. White and aimless signals. No
One listens to poetry.

Spicer begins his book *Language* with this poem, but it is a poem that is intended to end much more than it begins. What it means to end is Spicer's conception of himself as a poet—a lyric subject—something he is never finally capable of doing. Furthermore, it is meant to silence the profane desire to communicate through poetry by opening itself to the negation of its purportedly social intention: "No one listens to poetry." As soon as the poem admits this point, it achieves a state of "aimlessness" like that of the ocean, its unattainable model—and promptly ceases to exist as utterance. The poem as pure signal, never to be received, never to be comprehended: mutely gesturing to themselves as harbingers of some linguistic equivalent of the Messianic Kingdom (what the poet calls in an early piece "some great Catalina of a dream / Out where the poem ends"), Spicer's poems, in themselves, can never be redeemed.

V

Only the intensive directing of the words into the kernel of the innermost silence will achieve true action.
        —Walter Benjamin (in a letter to Martin Buber)

We have come to give you metaphors for poetry.
        —Told to W. B. Yeats

Anyone who takes up the study of Messianism quickly recognizes the drastic ambivalence with which this body of ideas is charged. Scholem himself, in whom one finds both revolutionary and conservative attitudes, seems of two minds in this regard: whereas he recognizes and even celebrates the vitalizing power of Messianic yearning, like the true dialectician he also sees the psycho-historical perils it represents, especially as it has been put into practice in the course of Jewish history. Whether this situation also applies here, in the realm of metaphoric poetics, remains to be seen. The pressures placed upon a poet are not necessarily those placed upon a social movement, and it is just at the point of recognizing the real historical dangers of pressing for the End that my elaborate metaphor may break down. I will only note one particularly exciting observation in Scholem's work as a potential point of departure for further discussion: "The aggressiveness, the revolutionary element which is part and parcel of the Messianic movements, was bound to scare away the bearers of authority. In turning itself against the status quo, such a movement also called into question its subjection to the existing structure of traditional forms. . . . The more intensive the outbreak and the larger the arena in which such a movement took place, the more clearly was a new situation created in which traditional exegeses were no longer as important as the confrontation with historical realities."

This leads me to my final set of speculations, for although my own Messianism is a movement of one, it certainly presents me with the inadequacy of traditional exegeses when confronting historical realities. There are poems which can be seen as emanations, as the early Kabbalists saw God's act of creation. The emanations of the *Sefiroth* from the hidden world of deity, the appearance of positive qualities out of Nothing, have often struck me as a way to view those poems which seem to pour forth their bounty, moving from one image-world to the next in a celebration of linguistic plenitude. Silence is driven back in the face of such utterance and the poem resonates long after its formal closure. In contrast to this model we have the Lurianic Kabbalah, with its crucial notion of contraction, *Tsimtsum,* in which emanation occurs in a more problematic fashion, only after God has withdrawn into himself to make a space for creation. Lurianic Kabbalah is more charged with the Messianic spirit; and I have argued that the poem which presses for the End likewise withdraws into itself, opening itself to silence as it leaps to its closure, for it cannot sustain itself as utterance in the grip of its Messianic longing.

These then are two related paradigms for poetic composition; and as I have pointed out, I believe that some of our most significant poets, no doubt reacting to our culture's inability to produce valid positive image-worlds, have in various ways written their poems in accordance with the latter model. Very few poets today can write the poem of plenitude; and if so many poems today strike me as false, it is due to the inflated utterance of these misguided attempts. Neither emanation nor contraction, these poems, with their self-indulgent rhetoric, their quiveringly personal sensibilities, are the shells, the *Kelipot* that are the exfoliations of the processes of creation. Indeed, poetry today is a prisoner in the realm of the *Kelipot.* Who will lift up the broken sparks of the original image-worlds and begin the act of *Tikkun,* our much needed Restoration?

POSTSCRIPT

Once I thought that our most sublime moments, the moments when we are most in touch with ourselves and all that has produced us, could be rendered into art when, out of our desire, we gave ourselves up wholly to "the voice of language itself." But there is another voice we must sometimes heed, and that voice never utters a word. We speak, and in speaking create endless models of discourse that echo back at us and bid us respond. One great model, the model of Messianic discourse that through both art and religion was once heard so plainly, is now so distant from us that it returns only as silence. Sometimes it bears down upon us, and we rush to welcome it, receive it with open arms. And in the extremity of its embrace we too fall silent.

PROJECT AND UTTERANCE

In recent years, I have come to value art that risks sentimentality, art that barely touches the sentimental. For a long time I thought of myself as an enemy of sentimentality; to indulge in such feeling-states was to find oneself a long way down the road to kitsch. I still believe this, but when I find myself lured by the music of Schubert, immersed in the stories of I. B. Singer, or captivated by films like *Fanny and Alexander* or *Wings of Desire,* I know that the wholehearted ambivalence I have always felt toward my own interior realm of nostalgia is making itself felt. Much of this has to do with my love of fantasy and magic, the original childhood means of coping with the threats of the adult world, which not only impose themselves from without but grow steadily from within as well. From early readings of fairy tales and mythology, to a deep love of Coleridge, Shelley and Keats, to encounters with Freud and Robert Duncan's *The Truth & Life of Myth,* I have gradually learned the powers of the sentimental, the images and peculiar affects to which it is assigned, the pleasures and dangers it offers. It provides a sense of the magic of the self which other artistic registers, dependent upon more mature feeling-states, cannot. Eliot's extinction of personality and all the claptrap of the pseudo-scientific modernists have held me from time to time, but subconsciously I have always known that such was not for me: "I hear it in the deep heart's core." Criticism needs the objective sensibility so cherished by the modernists, and in becoming a critic I somehow must have felt I was paying my dues to intellectual powers that had granted me insights that I still value today. Yet I was at first and always have been a poet, and despite the dubious sociological role assigned to such a figure, my archetype can still be found in the concluding lines of "Kubla Khan" or "Ode to the West Wind." The prophetic authority that the poet desires is akin to the magical powers for which the child so longs; and both are sentimental expressions of thwarted and blocked subjectivity.

All this surely comes forth now for its own sake, but I am also concerned with the state of poetry today, or more precisely (though it may sound absurd), with the state of the poet's soul. I take my renewed fascination with the risks of sentimentality to be a sign of my increasingly defensive attitude toward what I consider to be unwarranted incursions upon the poet's right to inwardness. Poetry is no longer the exclusive literary domain of inwardness, and only at rare moments in its history has it been an exclusively inward art. But only a richly developed interior life can produce poetic utterance, which remains, however, rarely heard today, the hidden birthright of every true poet.

Utterance issues forth in the language of subjective authority, although such authority is never directly willed into being. Rather, it appears to be bestowed upon poets at those moments when they are deeply immersed in their inner lives, when they are caught up in negotiating those paths which lead to their most personal, even idiosyncratic psychic states. Because of their vulnerability at such moments (for they see their inadequacies along with their strengths), poets are always preparing themselves as they make their way: they develop a style through which utterance can make itself heard, and an inner world which can provide the scenes for such linguistic events. This may take some time, or it may occur at a stroke. Here is a modern instance; the scene is set, the self at its most peculiar is approached, and the voice booms forth, sounding itself at its creation:

> Not less because in purple I descended
> The western day through what you called
> The loneliest air, not less was I myself.
>
> What was the ointment sprinkled on my beard?
> What were the hymns that buzzed beside my ears?
> What was the sea whose tide swept through me there?

Out of my mind the golden ointment rained,
And my ears made the blowing hymns they heard.
I was myself the compass of the sea:

I was the world in which I walked, and what I saw
Or heard or felt came not but from myself;
And there I found myself more truly and more strange.

Is this a birth? A strangely wrought memory of the sense of identity revealed in childhood? A declaration of self-sufficiency madly pitched beyond the range of ordinary human sympathy? In the end, I believe it matters very little. "Tea at the Palaz of Hoon" may risk megalomania in its broadcast of the heroic ego, the subject as god-king, but in doing so it recovers a linguistic authority that remains unsurpassed in our time. It breaks through the lush and exotic sets of the early Stevens even as it definitively focuses them. Because the poet is reaching beyond himself, the poem borders on the grotesque. Nevertheless, there is no apparent strain either verbally or psychically; the overall effect is of the slow, sure accumulation of a vast interior power, the simultaneous creation and release of a mighty reservoir of poetic invention. The result is as purely triumphant a poem as can be written under modern conditions, which accounts, of course, for its noticeable brevity.

Like the Romantic poet-prophets who precede him, the god-king of Stevens's poem wishes to be the least sentimental of figures, for only a truly unsentimental voice, a voice which has freed itself from nostalgic loss and regret, can have the self-sufficiency to declare "I was the world in which I walked." The use of the past tense is revealing: the poem memorializes itself as it comes into being, casting itself backward into the western day, when the setting sun sent forth golden rays to anoint the obsessive figure standing alone in the purple air of twilight. This moment is gone, but the poem calls it back; thus the poem achieves its thorough and serene presence. In its relation to its own past, the poem is utterly nostalgic and sentimental, but verbally it treats its sentimental matter with palpable dispassion. This doubleness of attitude is confirmed in the articulation of the last line: "And there I found myself more truly and more strange."

Modern poetic utterance is closely bound up in the enactment of such doubleness: it is dialectical in its relation to its matter and its presentation of itself as verbal entity. As confident assertion, it puts itself forward; but such an authoritative gesture cannot be unambivalent. In "My Mother Would Be A Falconress," Robert Duncan describes these circumstances with poignant beauty:

> Ah, but high, high in the air I flew.
> And far, far beyond the curb of her will,
> were the blue hills where the falcons nest.
> And then I saw west to the dying sun—
> it seemd my human soul went down in flames.

The humanity of the soul must be sacrificed so that it may enter fully into its poetic estate. I do not mean that one must give up one's humanity to become a poet—quite the contrary! But what is necessary is the loss of the direct and immediate response to all that is comfortable and familiar: if I may conflate the two poems I have cited for a moment, in the blue hills where the falcons nest, one finds oneself more truly and more strange. But the price of such an uncanny sense of the self, and of the verbal resources needed to articulate that sense, is the restless guilt and nostalgic longing which may be heard speaking with and against the proud utterance of poetic identity:

> My mother would be a falconress,
> and even now, years after this,
> when the wounds I left her had surely heald,
> and the woman is dead,
> her fierce eyes closed, and if her heart
> were broken, it is stilld.
>
> I would be a falcon and go free.
> I tread her wrist and wear the hood,
> talking to myself, and would draw blood.

Few poets are capable of sustaining the verbal intensity generated by such psychic doubleness, for in doing so they put themselves at constant risk. I am not thinking now of the risks taken in confessional poetry, when the ego, upon appearing to itself in its bleakest guises, proves too vulnerable to such overheated images and disintegrates into melodrama. As I have argued, utterance involves dispassion in the treatment of the self as well as minute sensitivity to emotional nuances: one knows oneself truly only as a stranger. But consider instead the chance the poet takes in lines such as these:

> I am William Bronk, have been raised to believe
> the personal pronoun plus the verb to be
> and a proper name said honestly is fact
> from which the plainest narrative begins.
> But it isn't fact; it comes to this. Is it wrong?
> Not wrong. Just that it isn't true.
> No more than the opposite is true.

No golden ointment here, and no blue hills. But this is utterance nonetheless. All of us are sentimentally attached to "the plainest narrative," and it takes a tremendous will and doubtful strength to simultaneously embrace it and call it into question. When the self is cast into doubt, ambivalence becomes a source of great verbal power. The poet taken out of himself, for whom the ordinary grammatical construction of identity loses its familiar comfort and is made strange, recognizes instead a more powerful identity in otherness and unknowing. In the case of Bronk's "The Plainest Narrative," the result is a weird gaiety, almost nonchalant:

> . . . Do as you will.
> It doesn't matter. What happens to us is not
> what happens. It isn't by us. We feel it there.
> Listen. Something is living. It is not we.

Strangely enough, Bronk's poem reminds me of Emily Dickinson's "After great pain, a formal feeling comes—." Though the two pieces are worlds apart in tone (Dickinson's ritualized dread, Bronk's studied casualness), I believe that they both emerge from a crisis of the self, a simultaneous and conflictive awareness of both personal insignificance and subjective power which leads in turn to a sudden poetic outpouring, hard won in its autonomy. The severity of Dickinson's "Hour of Lead" is almost too much to bear, but bear it she does, and passes on its memory to us: it is the hour of the poem. After great pain, a *formal* feeling comes: not only do the nerves sit ceremonious, but the words do as well. The poem may entomb the self, recollecting a time of near total psychic annihilation, but such are the risks which the poet sometimes must take. The poem resurrects the self, calls it back from death, names it, tells its story. But it is not the poem's story. The poem is speaking from an impossible distance, and regardless of what it is saying, its utterance resounds: I Am That I Am.

My invocation of Emily Dickinson leads me to some of my most troubled thoughts about modern poetry. My tastes are conditioned by long residence in richly endowed worlds of feeling, aesthetic states nurtured by elaborate sentiment. If occasionally I appear to be attracted to small or meager work, it is because I sense the grandeur and plenitude of utterance looming just behind an apparently modest facade. "Tell all the Truth but tell it slant—." Dickinson's instructions to herself, her reliance on "Circuit" as the means of attaining to dazzling verbal power, lead her to a portentous set of strategies which, although triumphant within the boundaries she describes for herself, has very different results for her modern followers.

Dickinson's recent popularity is due in part to an understanding of her poetry as an ongoing project, an open-ended act of writing. In Dickinson, we confront a steady process of accretion under the self-consciously engineered conditions of her daily life; therefore some of her readers today have argued that the proper way to encounter the work is through nothing less than its totality. To some extent, this is an admirable proposition: a great poet must be read in her entirety, especially by those who feel they are following in her footsteps. But I would argue that the open-ended quality in Dickinson's work that is so admired today for its own sake is also—and perhaps more importantly—the means by which she comes to authoritative speech:

Mine—by the Right of the White Election!
Mine—by the Royal Seal!
Mine—by the Sign in the Scarlet prison—
Bars—cannot conceal!

Mine—here—in Vision—and in Veto!
Mine—by the Grave's Repeal—
Titled—Confirmed—
Delirious Charter!
Mine—long as Ages steal!

Poems such as this are both project and utterance. Given the contours of Dickinson's life—a life designed exclusively for the production of poetry—we can understand this text as a crucial moment of consolidation in the process of identity as well as a major statement in its own right. Perhaps we can fully appreciate the White Election poem only in the context of Dickinson's complete career. Nevertheless, the rhetoric of the poem is of such force that it also distinguishes itself from the ongoing project, and from the many other great poems of which that project is largely constituted.

The cultural project looms large in the self-conception of many modern poets. Americans are particularly attracted to the idea, given that Dickinson and Whitman are their progenitors. (Many of the same observations I have made regarding Dickinson could be made of Whitman as well.) If a European cognate is desired, one need look no further than Baudelaire and *Les Fleurs du Mal.* In all of these poets, project and utterance achieve an exemplary balance. The individual poem stands forth against the backdrop of the general work. If we are in the midst of the project, we are simultaneously aware of its exterior purpose, its intellectual motivation acting through a moving temporal structure, and the sudden cessation of temporal movement, the gathered force of privileged sentiment:

La très-chêre était nue, et, connasssant mon coeur,
File n'avait garde que ses bijoux sonores,

Dont le riche attirail lui donnait l'air vanqueur
Qu'ont dans leurs jours heureux les esclaves des Mores.

My darling was naked, or nearly, for knowing my heart
she had left on her jewels, the bangles and the chains
whose jingling music gave her the conquering air
of a Moorish slave on the days her master is pleased.

("Les Bijoux," trans. Richard Howard)

The shock of that opening quatrain as it emerges from the ongoing erotic procedures of *Les Fleurs du Mal* is as strong now as when I first read the poem. No wonder it was censored! This is a moment of erotic intensity that sheds light on Baudelaire's entire enterprise. Even the sustained rhyme testifies to the strength of the utterance.

The problem that I perceive in much of the most ambitious modern poetry stems from a failure to consistently achieve this simultaneity of project and utterance. It is obvious in especially long works variously conceived as open forms: *The Cantos, Paterson, The Maximus Poems,* and *"A"* all contain vast arid tracts, and I think that even the dedicated reader meets the prospect of going through these poems from start to finish with chagrin. Their more ardent defenders usually admit that the need to read them in their entirety depends upon some understanding of the poet's project, the conceived plan of the work as it interacts with the continuity of composition, congruent with the shape of a life over time. Though I find moving passages in all of these poems, I consider such defenses less and less convincing. The poets who take on these projects rarely lose sight of their original intentions (at times I wish that this occurred more often!), but I feel that too frequently the project in itself becomes the only rationale for its continuity—as if the exterior act of writing over time comes to dominate the poet, whatever the real degree of engagement might be with the materials under hand.

As a part of this tradition, Duncan too falls prey to what could be described as a reified notion of process. Too much of his poetry, especially in his last books, seems to be written out of a misguided attempt to endlessly illuminate the "orders" or coherences of the verbal, the

natural, and the imaginative. Although these orders in themselves constitute Duncan's greatest theme, their endless play proves to be an
insufficient basis for poetry: of equal necessity is an awareness of event,
of consequence, which arrests the process, concentrates its elements,
and thereby confirms its significance. By contrast, Bronk intuitively
understands the formal need for such a dialectical interplay. As he says
in "2+2 (=1?)":

> Now, I want to say oh, God, yes
> these impossible poems, crude and diverse:
> what had you thought to say or didn't you think?
> I guess didn't plan them as a sequence. I took
> them one at a time the way they came. Maybe they don't
> add; we keep looking for whatever does.

What we may assume to be a sequence, a continuous project driven by
certain philosophical concerns and verbal attitudes, also proves to be
discrete, disjunctive moments of utterance, "impossible" in their resistance to any systematized process of composition. All that remains constant, continual in its restlessness, is the search for what adds up—a
constancy which is disrupted by each new beginning, each new verbal
event.

But is it possible to come to each new poem as to a birth, a constant imitation of that great recitation with which Genesis begins? Can
each poem declare itself apart from what precedes it, yet somehow
enriched by the knowledge of what came before?

> . . . thou from the first
> Wast present, and, with mighty wings outspread,
> Dove-like sat'st brooding on the vast Abyss,
> And mad'st it pregnant . . .

Harold Bloom asserts that Milton's God brooding over the Abyss is an
image of the poet himself brooding over his poem, so that "the account
of Creation in Genesis has become a Midrash upon Milton." I can well
believe it, and am almost convinced therefore that with the gradual loss

of such authority, poetry is irredeemably fallen and is falling still. Often I look about me with pain and frustration, seeking the poets of my own generation who have neither trivialized the self through the dull recounting of mundane life nor have utterly dismantled the self in the vain belief that its presence is a hindrance to their verbal play. Perhaps it is true, as some theorists tell us, that our experience of the self, especially as it is manifested in poetry, is nothing more than a linguistic construction, a trope in a sentence written by any of a number of the windy abstractions that social scientists love to name. Such knowledge may be of occasional use to me as a critic, but as a poet I would as soon forget it. Like so much of the other noise that fills our heads these days, it keeps us from that listening silence, that act of attention which is also a place, a place, as Stevens says, "Where the voice that is in us makes a true response."

STATEMENT AND COMMENTARY

Poetry as statement, poetry as commentary: let us consider them as two complementary attitudes toward poetic composition, two distinct modes of poetic discourse. I noticed them first as tendencies in my own work, but have observed them in much modern poetry as well. A consideration of modern poetry in these terms may prove a worthwhile alternative to analyses of genre (lyric, narrative, dramatic monologue and so on), for the closer we come to the present, the less adequate such standard categories become in our attempts at description and evaluation. The same is true for debates over techniques (the use of rhyme and meter, of prose versus lineation, of fragmented syntax, etc.), which have become so overheated of late that the relative strengths and weaknesses of all poetic devices are temporarily obscured. Poetry regarded as statement or commentary is neither a matter of genre nor technique. Broadly speaking, it is a matter of rhetoric, since the poem's movement between the poles of statement and commentary must be mapped according to its figures or tropes. I suspect, however, that this mapping would lead in turn to an interpretation of poetic sensibility, an old-fashioned notion following the death (or disintegration) of the author, but one which, I contend, is still of use.

The sensibility that stands behind a poem exists prior to the act of composition, though we perceive it in the composition, resulting, as it were, as a by-product of linguistic form. It need not be identified with an authorial self, but on the other hand, it is not constructed of the relationship between the poem and exterior social forces. A poetic sensibility is created in the space between self and form; it is the measure of the poet's responsiveness, or as George Steiner says, *answerability*, to the conditions of being. According to Steiner, "The authentic experience of understanding, when we are spoken to by another human being or by a poem, is one of responding responsibility." Thus, for the purposes of this essay, the poem must be described psychologically and stylistically, for it partakes equally of psyche and *poesis*. (Granted, the psyche itself may be constituted as a language, but it is not a made or styled entity as is a poem.)

This is why a consideration of the poem as statement and commentary offers the kind of flexibility that is wanting in many recent discussions of modern poetry: as criticism intended to ascertain the nature of poetic sensibility, it will eclipse neither language nor self. Nor would such a consideration preclude a rigorous historical understanding of the poem: as a psycholinguistic entity, a poetic sensibility cannot be comprehended except in relation to history, against which it must be dialectically juxtaposed. Indeed, as I hope to show, statement and commentary are themselves historically conditioned terms, and may lead to a greater understanding of a poet's historical significance.

As a model of poetry as statement, here is poem 536 of Emily Dickinson:

> The Heart asks Pleasure—first—
> And then—Excuse from Pain—
> And then—those little Anodynes
> That deaden suffering—
>
> And then—to go to sleep—
> And then—if it should be
> The will of the Inquisitor
> The privilege to die—

The language of the poem is boldly direct and concise, strikingly spare, and at first glance, oddly free of figuration. "The Heart," of course, is a traditional symbol for the seat of the emotions, the capacity for feeling. In this instance, presumably, it is a synecdoche for "the individual" or even "I," but in its series of unadorned requests, it takes on a literalness that is appropriate to its singular emotive power. This series of requests is itself almost uncanny in its orderliness, and in the "logic" of that order: if not pleasure, then at least no pain; if pain, then at least those little anodynes; if no anodynes, then at least sleep; if no sleep, then at least death. The sequence is appalling, and no less for the tone of calm self-control as it is traced out than for the resignation and fatality that it adumbrates.

As in many of Dickinson's most wrenching poems, there is a sense that the text of #536 has been composed in—or as—the aftermath to unspeakable shock. The "Inquisitor" (to whom I would relate the "Goblin" torturer of poems 414 and 512, written the same year) administers that shock, and then, in overseeing the composition, serves as a sadistic muse. But whereas most of these poems of psychic torment tend to phantasmagoria—Dickinson's "Maelstrom, with a notch" or elemental torture wrack—#536 relies on what could be called a grammar of linearity, a structure of accretive statement which is one of Dickinson's most significant poetic accomplishments.

A similar approach may be seen in a less familiar poem with a very different mood, #1354:

> The Heart is the Capital of the Mind—
> The Mind is a single State—
> The Heart and the Mind together make
> A single Continent—
>
> One—is the Population—
> Numerous enough—
> This ecstatic Nation
> Seek—it is Yourself.

The old allegorical figure of the self as state takes on the same strange literalness which we observed in #536. But in this case, however, the poem consists not of a series of statements about the figure ("The Heart asks . . ."), but of the development or working-through of the figure. The fierce Emersonian ending of the poem comes almost as the conclusion of a syllogism or the answer to a riddle. But since it is also cast in the imperative ("Seek—"), the statement takes on both urgency and authority, affects which are enhanced by "This ecstatic Nation." This is the most emotionally charged phrase in the poem; it is also the goal which the reader (or the poet, if she is speaking to herself) is urged to seek. The poem's statement-language is a representation of this process of self-discovery, and in this respect, the poem is a heuristic tool, an instrument with which one may attain to Dickinson's "single Continent," the unity of Heart and Mind. This ecstatic psychic state is inexpressible, for language is both inadequate and unnecessary when one has achieved so powerful a condition of self-reliance. Thus the poem ends—and ends with a sense of resolute closure—as it enters into that condition. A similar poem, #1056, which uses chronological rather than geographical tropes, likewise ends with the declaration that "Consciousness—is Noon."

Dickinson's language of statement can thus represent the extremes of sensibility. It can adumbrate a process of centering and assertion, or of loss and dissolution. Today we think of Dickinson as one of the first great modern poets, a view that is derived, at least in part, from her original combination of penetrating psychological insight and startling economy of linguistic means. Regardless of her subject matter—a natural phenomenon, a civic or domestic event, an emotional state, a religious experience—Dickinson's poems are always (in)formed by a desire to totally *comprehend* psychological implications and, at the same time, radically *condense* verbal expression. At first glance, the result often appear straightforward, but a closer look reveals how oblique, how multivalent Dickinson's language can become. As she tells us in poem 1071,

> Perception of an object costs
> Precise the Object's loss—
> Perception in itself a Gain
> Replying to its Price—
> The Object Absolute—is nought—
> Perception sets it fair
> And then upbraids a Perfectness
> That situates so far—

The degree to which we perceive the object equals the degree to which the object is lost. But to whom? To itself? Dickinson cannot imagine that this can be the case: "The Object Absolute—is nought—/Perception sets it fair." Arguably, the object exists only because we perceive it (even if, as might be the case here, the "Object Absolute" is God). On the other hand, our perception "upbraids" a perfect existence that is utterly apart from us, that we cannot truly perceive, that has no need to be perceived by the human subject. Perception, then, seems to be both an immensely powerful instrumentality and a wholly inadequate one; the poem, ending with that teasing dash, seems incapable of coming to a decision. As Dickinson's literary descendant, William Bronk, will say some hundred years later, "What else but the mind/senses the final uselessness of the mind?"

Perception of the object, of course, must precede writing about it. Moving from perception of the object to verbal representation of such perception results in yet another loss; as Bronk understands, the poem, as an approach to the object, will prove even more oblique, no matter how plain and direct a statement it seeks to make. The best practitioners of a poetry of statement are constantly aware of this. Their psychological and epistemological acuity obligate a rhetoric and a grammar of direct engagement that will sooner or later admit their undermined and thwarted purposes. In the case of Dickinson, the great range of her concerns (a range which, despite her canonic status, has only recently been recognized) and the audacity of her declarative power mark her as the unsurpassed master of this poetic mode, a mode which perfectly suits the sensibility of this "Vesuvian" recluse. Yet such mastery is really, both socially and poetically, an anti-mastery; as Susan Howe observes, she was able "To find affirmation in renunciation and to be (herself) without." Or as Dickinson herself would have it, "I dwell in Possibility—/A fairer House than Prose—."

In recent examples of poetry as statement, we find two rhetorical tendencies, both of which are already operative in the Dickinson poems we have considered. These tendencies are by no means mutually exclusive (there are poems in which both may be observed), but should be considered the two likely results of a poetry determined to directly engage and investigate its subject matter, and plainly articulate or verbally enact those processes. On the one hand, the poem can proceed straightforwardly, undeterred by any self-consciousness in regard to its instrumentalities of knowledge and utterance. The poem will take its form and seek its end with the determinate simplicity that has always been associated with the lyric genre. (Think of the first of Dickinson's poems we considered, #536.) On the other hand, the poem may immediately, nearly upon the outset, make its self-consciousness the very subject matter itself: if there is any other ostensible subject matter, it will give way quickly, so that the poem becomes a discourse on its own making, the powers and limitations thereof. (Consider the last of the Dickinson poems in our discussion, #1071.) As I have said, these tendencies are not mutually exclusive, for it would be a rare modern poem cast in the mode of a statement that did not at least to some extent consider itself in its encounter with the subject, and make itself part of that subject, however distant from the subject the utterance might seem to be.

Here, however, is a poem that turns very little in this way; rhetorically speaking, it is quite determined in its straightforward expression, and its power lies in its assertiveness, despite the uncertainty that is its subject matter. The poem is Robert Creeley's "Mind's Heart":

> Mind's heart, it must
> be that some
> truth lies locked
> in you.
>
> Or else lies, all
> lies, and no man
> true enough to know
> the difference.

This is a poem that is *certain of its uncertainty*. Unlike a great deal of Creeley's work, which is often regarded as hesitant or tentative in its utterance, "Mind's Heart" presents itself with an almost blunt confidence. What is the "mind's heart"? This odd locution, which serves as the poem's title and is then immediately repeated in the first line, takes us back to Dickinson's "The Heart is Capital of the Mind," a truth which must be recognized on the path toward self-discovery. And indeed, for Creeley as well, "it must/be that some/truth lies locked/in you." But Creeley, whose conception of the self is far less stable than his precursor's, in the next stanza reverses his assertion: there are nothing but lies locked in the mind's heart, and no one is capable of determining inner truth from falsehood.

This despairing skepticism, however, is presented with an immediacy and sureness that transforms doubt into a simple existential truth. The conviction of Creeley's statement-language may best be observed in his line breaks, especially in the poem's second stanza. Creeley enjambs the most important phrases, resulting in a rhythmic and semantic emphasis that would be lost if the lineation of the stanza followed the conventional grammatical units in an end-stopped fashion. Note the tension produced by "all/lies," "no man/true enough" and "to know/the difference." This emphatic lineation is the formal correlative to Creeley's epistemological assertiveness: we know that we cannot know the truth of the mind's heart; that much at least we can state with certainty.

"Love Comes Quietly," written during the same period (1959-1960) employs another of Creeley's typical techniques, a casual, off-handed rhyme, in order to soften the impact of the assertion. Here, the lyric impulse is given more freedom, and the statement is suffused with the wistful humility that is often associated with Creeley's love poetry:

> Love comes quietly,
> finally, drops
> about me, on me,
> in the old ways.
>
> What did I know
> thinking myself
> able to go
> alone all the way.

Creeley's poetic project (like Dickinson's) consists of a life-long tracking of the self. It requires continual vigilance and a finely tuned recording ability, an awareness of circumstances which always consists, in part, of language. Creeley's short, nervous lines are the result of this immediate awareness, which also entails a splitting of the poetic sensibility. There is the one who experiences, there is the one who writes, and they are not altogether congruent. But there are moments when "love comes quietly." They are moments of release, of grace, when the self is made whole by the presence of the beloved, the annealing other whose entrance into the poet's world must be acknowledged with the utmost simplicity and a singleness of purpose intended as a form of homage and thanksgiving. Without the beloved, the poetic project cannot continue; as Creeley admits, he is not "able to go/alone all the way."

The balance that Creeley is able to achieve between vexing self-consciousness and the healing balm of love is seen at its most beautiful in "The Rain." Here, doubt and assurance produce a sort of verbal dance, a pattern of observations that turn inward and outward until the poem comes to rest. "What am I to myself," Creeley asks, "that must be remembered,/insisted upon/so often?" The anxiety represented by this question drives the poem forward. "Locked in this/final uneasiness," the poet longs to be free of himself, seeing in the rain, with which he associates the beloved, the ease that comes to the self only in the other's presence. The address to the beloved with which the poem ends records the poet's hard-won success: not a loss of self, but an acceptance of the self as it finds its place with the other, though it is a place which the poet can only hope he will be granted:

> Love, if you love me,
> lie next to me.
> Be for me, like rain,
> the getting out
>
> of the tiredness, the fatuousness, the semi-
> lust of intentional indifference.
> Be wet
> with a decent happiness.

"Properly no verse should be called a poem," says Louis Zukofsky, Creeley's mentor, "if it does not convey the totality of perfect rest." The erotic fulfillment so plainly and yet so craftily stated at the end of "The Rain" is surely one version of that totality.

But now consider this poem, the last of our examples of poetry as statement:

> We know, now, who it all was though, of course,
> we always knew. What good did it do to know
> or to think we knew? We could as well say,
> "It wasn't anyone," for all we know.
>
> And that would be true. Once we have in mind
> what there is to talk about, whatever we say
> is all right; it doesn't matter what we say
> or even if we don't find anything to say.

William Bronk's "The Unsaid" is taken up solely with its self-consciousness, and makes of it something quite different from Creeley's "uneasiness." Instead of drawing the poet's discourse toward the rested totality of the beloved, a frustrated awareness of human limitations, especially of linguistic limitations, produces and consumes the poem's discourse entirely. Granted, this is an extremely abstract poem, even for Bronk, who is a master of verbal abstraction. Bronk usually proceeds by first naming a specific circumstance or object and then venturing increasingly abstract statements, until it becomes clear that the original matter of the poem was a mere premise for the subsequent establishment of poetry (or, Poetry) as universal discourse. But in this instance, I have deliberately selected a poem that completely lacks what is conventionally understood as the basic material of poetry, that is, imagery. Here Bronk relies on the tensile strength of his syntax, for the poem is at all points a resistance to "the unsaid," which is arguably the true subject matter of all his poems.

The unsaid is the absolute which lies outside human existence, before which all we are, all we know, and all we can say, are as nothing.

Traditionally, we have named this absolute "God," but given Bronk's radical agnosticism, "We could as well say,/'It wasn't anyone.'" We can only intuit this, and when we attempt to describe our situation in relation to the unsaid, we find ourselves speaking about the limits of language. All talk becomes the same; all statements regarding our condition are equally valid; and silence carries as much significance as speech. With this recognition, the poem's statement-language closes down. Dickinson's poems often end with the discovery of the self, and Creeley's with the discovery of the beloved. But Bronk's poems frequently end with the discovery that poetic utterance is incommensurate with its ultimate subject matter. In Bronk's view, poetry (like self-reliance, or like love) can be a great consolation. Because human desire is infinite, poetry continues to be written; we can never cease making statements about human experience, however limited and contradictory those statements prove to be. But we do so with the equally powerful knowledge of our finitude, a knowledge through which the utterance of every single poem is finally overthrown. Thus poetry is always a prelude to silence.

The sensibility which tends toward a poetry of statement is a sensibility struggling to come to terms with its finitude; it is a psyche that is resentful of and offended (but still fascinated by) the knowledge of its inevitable death. It is, as Keats says, "half in love with easeful Death," or as in Bronk's "Evaluation," "It wants a death and waits on the street for it." This knowledge of finitude and death has been discovered in isolation; indeed, the existential condition of a true poetry of statement is that of isolation, of loss of connectedness, of ambivalence toward any notion of communion or continuity. Love poetry does not come easily to such a sensibility, nor does a poetry overtly concerned with other types of social intercourse. The poem reaches out to the distant contours of the other only with great difficulty, impeded by doubts about the worth of social contact and by strong instincts toward self-preservation, the desire to remain intact and unchanged. According to Freud in *Beyond the Pleasure Principle*, these instincts "are bound to give a deceptive appearance of being forces tending towards change and progress, whilst in fact they are merely seeking to reach an ancient goal by paths alike old and new." That ancient goal is, of course, the inanimate, the closure of death.

Poetically, the result of such forces is always the highest degree of linguistic compression, the most strikingly succinct speech. At its strongest, such a poetic sensibility glories in its visionary self-reliance, a power that will exhaust itself, leading back to oblivion. "The rest of life to *see!*" cries Dickinson. "Past Midnight! Past the Morning Star!" It is a declaration of self as world, of cosmic self-sufficiency, which Bronk confirms when he insists that "If I am anything at all, I am/the instrument of the world's passion." This instrument wants nothing but its fate, it exists to express that fate, which we in turn comprehend as our own.

But poetry as the instrument of the world's passion need not be derived only from conditions of isolation and self-reliance; it need not express its distrust of continuity in laconic measures and terse tropes. The passion of poetry—the passion that *is* poetry—may take form, may present itself, in the service of continuity. It entails a different order of rhetoric and a different poetic sensibility. I call such work a poetry of commentary because it is a poetry in which the engagement with the traditions of poetry and the other arts is most emphatic. Poetry as commentary is most sensitive to culture as an ongoing continuum. If poetry is that mode of language which is the fullest expression of psychic life, then I would speculate that a poetry of commentary stands in relation to Eros as a poetry of statement stands in relation to Thanatos. The purpose of Eros, says Freud in *Civlization and Its Discontents*, "is to combine human individuals, and after that families, then races, peoples and nations, into one great unity, the unity of mankind." In *The Sighted Singer*, Allen Grossman restates this theme in specifically poetic terms when he asserts that "When a poem is truly present in the world, it is present in the form of an interaction which is as profound and extensive as the social order itself."

In a certain respect, this interactive view applies to all poetry, since all poetry can bind people together in much the same way as Freud's Eros. But the type of poetry I have discussed up until now does so almost in spite of itself; its greatness lies partly in its austerity, the chastened assertions of its forms. As Bronk says in "The Nature of Musical

Form," "It is only fairness stating only itself." Poetry as commentary, on the other hand, tends to be a generous art, an art which actively seeks the other. Its fairness is derived by stating itself through another text, a pre-text which is also a mediating text, leading the poem to the completion of its utterance and serving as an integral part of the completed work. Obviously, the poem as commentary has something to say about a preexisting work, but it also intends the preexisting work as a paradigm of aesthetic, and hence of human relations. The new poem is an attempt to share in these relations, to participate in this model; thus it comes into form as an interaction, binding itself to and entering into dialogue with the earlier work and the tradition it represents.

Just as important for the new poem is the manner in which the earlier work has been rhetorically addressed, how it has been strategically appropriated so that the new poem can exist as an original entity. The new poem must be for itself as much as for the other; this strikes me as one of the essential truths of commentary as an interactive process, a function of Eros. In his *Summa Lyrica*, Grossman says of "appropriation" "that the interpretation of a text ends up in the self-interpretation of a subject who henceforth understands himself better." In poetry as commentary, the process of composition moves from textual interpretation to self-interpretation, from an understanding that is *of* a preexisting work to an understanding that *is* a new work. Because it bears this sign of commentary, it will invite its own future commentators, and its closure will always be tentative, however rich and full a discourse it may have achieved.

This concept must be distinguished from the broader and more pervasive notion of poetic influence. Whether one regards it as an Eliotic modification of an ideal order of monuments, or as a Bloomian struggle for priority against a threatening set of precursors, poetic influence takes part in the production of all poetry, regardless of the resulting rhetoric of the new poem. In the study of influence, all poetry is a poetry of commentary. The anthropomorphic bird which Dickinson encounters in poem 328, drinking "a Dew/From a convenient Grass" is a reworking of Keats's immortal nightingale that was "not born for death." In Eliot's terms, Keats's ode must always be understood in the retrospective light of Dickinson's naturalistic revision; in

Bloom's terms, Dickinson's swerve toward a figure of crude appetites and instinctive fears is a necessary curtailment of Keats's lofty, idealized singer. But Dickinson's rhetoric, as we have seen, is that of statement: in #328 she tracks the bird from point to point until it flies away. Keats's language, on the other hand, is more that of commentary, taking its inspiration from and sinuously embellishing a broad range of myths, artworks and cultural events, as well as specific texts of precursor poets, so as to gradually shape one of the most refined sensibilities in the history of poetry. There is no question that Keats stands behind Dickinson ("For Poets," she tells Higginson, "—I have Keats—and Mr. and Mrs. Browning"), but the resulting influence, however complex, still occurs between two distinctly different poetic sensibilities.

To see how the poem as commentary takes shape under Keats's hand, let us consider the sonnet "On Sitting Down to Read *King Lear* Once Again":

> O golden-tongued Romance with serene lute!
>> Fair plumed Syren! Queen of far away!
>> Leave melodizing on this wintry day,
> Shut up thine olden pages, and be mute:
> Adieu! for once again the fierce dispute
>> Betwixt damnation and impassion'd clay
>> Must I burn through; once more humbly assay
> The bitter-sweet of this Shakespearian fruit.
> Chief Poet! and ye clouds of Albion,
>> Begetters of our deep eternal theme,
> When through the old oak forest I am gone,
>> Let me not wander in a barren dream,
> But when I am consumed in the fire,
> Give me new Phoenix wings to fly at my desire.

This sonnet follows the basic paradigm of poetry as commentary: from textual interpretation to self-interpretation, from studying tradition to joining and revitalizing tradition. For Keats, poetic tradition consists of a number of greater and lesser strands. "Golden-tongued Romance" is silenced, at least temporarily, in the opening lines, as it is a "wintry day" and Romance is the milder genre of summer. "Romance," like "the old oak forest," is a term which Keats often associates with Spenser, and he is in process of revising *Endymion*, his own Spenserian forest, when he composes the sonnet. In returning to the wintry tragedy of *King Lear*, Keats seeks an altogether more severe and chastening encounter: "for once again the fierce dispute/Betwixt damnation and impassion'd clay/Must I burn through." These lines—the most powerful and most Shakespearian in the sonnet—encapsulate his thinking about the play. This "bitter-sweet" is the essence of the Shakespearian, and by extension, of the English poetic tradition; it is "our deep eternal theme."

The move from first-person singular to first-person plural in this line is of particular strategic importance: having specified the psychic power of the greatest English poetry, Keats enters its sphere; he binds himself to the tradition over which Shakespeare presides. (Keats to Haydon upon beginning *Endymion*: "I remember your saying that you had notions of a good Genius presiding over you—I have of late the same thought . . . Is it too daring to Fancy Shakespeare this Presider?") Consumed in the fire of *King Lear*, the poet knows he will win his "new Phoenix wings," for the sonnet, through the process of commentary, already has launched him at his desire. That desire is the writing of poetry, and while Keats understands that he cannot be Shakespeare, he senses now that he can be himself. "The excellence of every Art," he writes, "is its intensity, capable of making all disagreeables evaporate, from their being in close relationship to Beauty & Truth—Examine King Lear & you will find this examplified throughout." These lines, included in the same letter to his brothers in which Keats formulates his idea of negative capability, precedes the *King Lear* sonnet by about a month. To be sure, they apply to Shakespeare's tragedy. But the terms Keats uses, which will come to fruition in the great odes a scant two years later, are already his own.

When Keats's sonnet is read in relation to *King Lear*, it must be regarded as intensive commentary, concentrating and summarizing Keats's thought on the play even as it aligns him with the tradition and poetic values which Shakespeare is seen to represent. There is no other way for Keats to proceed: after all, he is working in a form which, however noted for its ability to condense great thoughts into a limited span, cannot compare to a work of such sheer magnitude. Furthermore, Keats is in awe of Shakespeare and his creation; he regards him as a kind of deity (he carries Shakespeare's portrait with him wherever he goes), and thinks of his work as a kind of second nature, replete with elemental forces such as the renewing fire that appears in the sonnet's penultimate line. The *King Lear* sonnet, then, is a good example of the type of commentary-poem that assumes a devotional stance toward its pre-text. The summarizing commentary we have just observed is appropriate to this stance: the new poem has only to touch briefly upon the matter of the pre-text for the new poem to establish, to utter, itself.

On the other hand, poems which regard their originating texts more as equals tend to be extensive commentaries; they expand, develop, fill in perceived gaps in the works which has come before. These are the poems that come closest to midrash. Like rabbinic commentators who regard a lacuna in a scriptural passage as an opportunity, secure in the belief, as Gershom Scholem puts it, that "revelation comprises everything that will ever be legitimately offered to interpret its meaning," some modern poets honor the text which inspires them by "opening" it to their expanded interpretive treatment. The poet's pre-text, like the rabbi's passage of Scripture, invites elaboration, for within its recesses are to be found the germinating ideas for new work.

Wallace Stevens' "Nuances of a Theme by Williams" is a clear example of a poem of this sort:

> *It's a strange courage*
> *you give me, ancient star:*
>
> *Shine alone in the sunrise*
> *toward which you lend no part!*

> I
>
> Shine alone, shine nakedly, shine like bronze,
> that reflects neither my face nor any inner part
> of my being, shine like fire, that mirrors nothing.

II
Lend no part to any humanity that suffuses
you in its own light.
Be not chimera of morning,
Half-man, half-star.
Be not an intelligence,
Like a widow's bird
Or an old horse.

Williams' brief lyric "El Hombre," with which Stevens begins his own poem, not only inspires Stevens but actually sets the tone of the piece, as if the second poem is composed in the "key" of the first. The title of Stevens' poem suggests that he is merely elaborating on a theme that is already quite apparent in "El Hombre."   Yet in doing so, Stevens not only extends Williams' idea but makes it very much his own—so much so that by the end of the piece, he has carried the theme so far, so quickly, that it is antithetical to Williams' usual poetic goals.

"El Hombre" ("The Man"), from Williams' volume *Al Que Quiere!* (1917) is not an altogether typical poem of that period. Although it is brief and direct in the imagist/objectivist manner, it has an abstract, symbolic quality, especially surrounding the "ancient star" which imparts courage to "El Hombre," the manly poet, heroic in his isolation. Just as the star shines alone in the sunrise toward which it lends no part—and which will render it invisible—so too the poets stands apart, certain of his invisibility despite his starry powers. He is apart from the world about which he sings, the common world of the streets and vacant lots, of the workers, housewives and sparrows which are already populating his other poems. In this poem, he recognizes himself as what Stevens will later call a figure of capable imagination, and it is for this reason that Stevens chooses to write a commentary-poem in response.

Stevens emphasizes the isolated courage in Williams' poem, the self-sufficiency of the star, and of the poet, who is answerable only to his fiery imagination. The star shines alone, nakedly, like bronze, like fire. It mirrors nothing, including, in its sublime indifference, the poet who invokes it. For Stevens, this is as it should be: the star must be entirely itself, and the same is true of the poet, who must also "Lend no part to any humanity that suffuses/you in its own light." By taking this theme further than Williams himself, Stevens produces a critical commentary on Williams' poetry of everyday events and common objects. Ordinarily, Williams' poetry is suffused in the light of quotidian humanity; it is just the kind of poetry of old horses and widows' birds which Stevens' starry poet rejects. Williams' "Hombre" is "Half-man, half-star"; Stevens, by contrast, wants a star—a poetic imagination—that is utterly itself, however surrounded it might be by the quotidian. Like the jar in Tennessee, it must not "give of bird or bush"; like the youthful rider in "Mrs. Alfred Uruguay," it must rush from the real to create "the ultimate elegance: the imagined land."

Thus, at a relatively early point in his career, Stevens uses the poem as commentary to define himself against a contemporary who shares many of his concerns but who finally assumes a stance that is the opposite of his own. Stevens is a good example of a poet who moves between statement and commentary. Longing for and at times achieving the radical isolation and compression of the poem as statement (as in, say, "The Snow Man" or "Tea at the Palaz of Hoon"), Stevens' work is typically more that of commentary. However he may insist on the autonomy of the imagination, he is always reminded by what has come before him and what surrounds him. Such awareness leads to the engagements and conflicts which largely comprise the body of his work.

One type of commentary poem that holds a special place in the tradition is poem addressed to a visual work of art. From "Ode on a Grecian Urn" to "Self-Portrait in a Convex Mirror," the greatest of these poems brood over the problematic nature of artistic power in its opposition to the inexorableness of passing time. A painting or a sculpture has substance. The facts of its material and spatial being, its obvious but always dangerous defiance of temporality, so crucial to its expressivity, make it a particularly tempting pre-text for poetry, which by contrast is a temporal art. Poems and musical compositions have no substance; they must be brought forth into time through reading or performance. Moving in time but plotting against it, they represent themselves as *significant time*. As George Steiner puts it in *Real Presences*,

"The time which music 'takes', and which it gives as we perform or experience it, is the only *free time* granted us prior to death." This is true of poetry to a lesser extent, since poetry, in that it is made of language rather than abstract tones, bears a referential burden from which music is largely free. A commentary-poem based on a piece of music thus runs a great risk of redundancy, and indeed, success ful poems based on musical works are few and far between. Not so with poems based on works of visual art, for poets know that painters and sculptors, allied with them against mortality, have means of expression which, in their overt materiality, lend themselves readily to both poetic mimesis and poetic abstraction.

John Hollander's "Ave Aut Vale" ("Either hale or farewell") is based on an untitled drawing by Saul Steinberg. In the drawing, three figures stand in a doorway. On the left, a man in a jacket and tie faces the viewer directly, while on the right stands a girl in a dress. Behind her a woman leans against the door frame; her face is turned toward the viewer as well. The figures are dressed in a nondescript mid-century style (the forties? the fifties?); they are compact, rather rectangular in build, with indefinite features. There is a certain child-like charm to the drawing, though the shading indicates great understanding and skill.

Hollander's poem—eighteen lines of syllabic verse—plays on the ambiguity of the drawing's relation to its viewer. Are we approaching the doorway, greeting the little group, or have we turned around for one last goodbye as we walk away? For Hollander, the space between the viewer and the people in the drawing is transformed into time, leading quickly and inevitably to an unfolding of the simple pathos inherent in the original work:

> 'Ah no, the years, the years . . .' While their image
> Was being taken from the only life
> They had, it was hard—wherever we were
> At that time ourselves—not to take umbrage
> At the way in which the shadows of all
> Our lives kept falling across the very
> Forms of those lives—shadows falling along

Doorsteps, reddened sands, desirable thighs,
Sighing water, responsive emulsions.

As is usually the case with Hollander's verse, the wordplay is tactful and refined: we "take umbrage" at the fact that a shadowy art will preserve the image of a peopled moment, while another Shadow obscures the human originals. Shadowed by implacable time, against which human desire is helpless, it is

> . . . hard not to find unbearable
> The way the images had been preserved:
> Not that method in itself but for the
> Mortality of the momentary
> Models.

This is the essence of lyric poetry's encounter with visual representation, especially of the human form. Centuries of poetic commentary lead to the same turn, the same conclusion. Confronted by art's continual present, poets elegize, protesting, consoling, but above all asserting their being. Empowered by their awareness of time, they articulate, they *temporize* the space of desire which mute art reveals. Steinberg's drawing bears the human image across time, while Hollander's commentary gives a voice to the pathos of that interminable journey. Such is the communal responsibility which a poetry of commentary assumes.

The consideration of poetry in terms of statement and commentary, as I said at the outset of this essay, may be of particular relevance to an understanding of modern poetry, which is why I have gone no further back than the early nineteenth century for my examples, and have made sure to discuss some much more recent poems. When regarded from the perspective of the arts, the historical crises of modernism and then of postmodernism produce a continual breaking of form. Keats was one of the very first poets to intuit this; for him, traditional forms and genres had a kind of contingency that was virtually unprecedented. This is why the poetic tradition manifests itself in his work through respectful but self-assertive commentary. To an even greater extent than the first generation of Romantics, Keats understood that "The Genius of Poetry must work out its own salvation in a man: It cannot be matured by law & precept, but by sensation & watchfulness in itself—That which is creative must create itself." For him, poets up through the Elizabethans were capable of fully mastering their art and could become "Emperors of vast Provinces," while his contemporaries—including Wordsworth, from whom he partly drew his conception of the self—were each of them, "like an Elector of Hanover [who] governs his petty state." Keats rejected this fate: as the Genius of Poetry works out its salvation through him, the result is a body of work that places the poetic sensibility's responsiveness to circumstance before any given body of artistic precepts and any preconceived notion of form.

The richness of style and intimacy of tone sustained throughout Keats' significant utterances are all the more remarkable given his brief, heterogeneous and often fragmentary career. But that career, influenced from without by poverty, disease and class prejudice, is influenced from within by a temperamental insistence on the congruence of beauty and truth which is to be achieved through whatever means the poet has at his disposal. The poetic sensibility must perceive each poem to be a justification of that congruence, at which point it is deemed complete—even when it appears to be abandoned. The *Hyperion* fragments tell us all we need to know about Keats' relation to *Paradise Lost*, just as his sonnet encapsulates his response to *King Lear*. They provide proof for his assertion that "A Man's life of any worth is a continual allegory," for in allegorizing his immense knowledge of and debt to the English poetic tradition, he brings that tradition to its culmination and dissolves it in his own inimitable style.

For Dickinson (with Keats' example before her), such means of coming into her own, despite its richness and generosity, was still unsuitable. An American and a woman, this self-elected "Empress of Calvary" apparently saw little point in the procedures of engagement and recapitulation that a poetry of commentary entails. "My business is circumference," she informs Higginson, meaning, as I understand it, an art which aims directly at the limits of discourse, with as few mediations as possible. Any attempt to contain her utterance would itself be contained, and those who would possess her be possessed:

> Circumference thou Bride of Awe
> Possessing thou shalt be
> Possessed by every hallowed Knight
> That dares to covet thee   (#1620)

In her essay on Dickinson, Adrienne Rich rightly associates her daemonic muse with Keats' "Genius of Poetry," though the salvation which that genius worked out through Dickinson was far more severe than that of her predecessor. Writing a poetry that is austere to the point of self-denial, Dickinson is our poet of life barely won from death, just as Keats is our poet of death grown forgetful of itself, intoxicated on the pleasures of life. Given the current state of poetry, a state in which discursive possibilities seem to be opening up and shutting down at a dizzying speed and contending literary ideologies endlessly redefine the boundaries of utterance, we have need of both modes in all their paradigmatic strengths.

In discussing the need of today's artists "to re-obtain fundamental ontological confidence," Allen Grossman observes that "It is a particular characteristic of the region of Postmodernism that the world seemed to have to be reconstructed as if from the beginning. That is why men and women of my generation are given to theory. Theory is the deep dream that precedes the description of a reality, the preconditions of which it constructs. There is, in other words, a primitivity that underlies the poetic motive of many writers in this age of theory."

This is an idea from which I am able to draw great confidence and encouragement. There are some poets today who have delved deeply into theory, and it has, perhaps, strengthened their art, sending it off into unanticipated directions. The results of such experiments are only now beginning to be judged. Other poets have decried the preponderance of theory, fearing that it has stolen a readership that rightfully belongs to them. This may be the case to some extent, though it behooves any poet who takes this position to produce a poetry—and a poetics—that is more compelling than the work of the theorists.

Grossman's notion of theory as the "deep dream" that precedes the reality of poetry, a sign, paradoxically, of the "primitivity" or earliness of our literary situation, compels in just this way. His poetry too has a kind of "primitivity"—though it is an immensely sophisticated art—that betokens a new earliness:

> I dreamed I sailed alone
> In a long boat, a white bone;
> Like a strong thought, or a right name
> The sail had no seam.

Sailing between the poles of statement and commentary, Grossman's "Ballad of the Bone Boat" is a poem which seems auratic in its sense of tradition but almost frightening in its sense of self. I urge my contemporaries to follow where it leads:

> The sea and the sky were one dark thing,
> The eye and the hand as cold.
> Unbound was my hair, unbound was my dress;
> Nothing beckoned or called
>
> But the words of a song
> That had death in its tune
> And death in its changes and close—
> A song which I sang in the eye of the moon,
> And a secret name that I chose.
>
> And this is the song: "Straight is the way
> When the compass is a stone,
> And the sail has no seam, and the boat is a bone,
> And the mast is bent like a tree that bears
> The wind-fruit of the moon."
>
> And now I sing, O come with me,
> And be at last alone;
> For straight is the way in the dream of the boat
> That is a long white bone.

TWO PROBLEMS
IN RECENT AMERICAN POETRY

I

The Self

The differences we can observe between the dominant poetic styles of two decades, the allegiances and critiques we derive therefrom, may not be the only or the most important ones, especially if our goal is a complex social understanding of poetry as a highly rarefied but abiding cultural discourse. The vicissitudes of the self in American poetry of the last twenty years serve as a case in point. Many poets have addressed themselves self-consciously to the status of the "lyric I," and critics such as Charles Altieri, Alan Williamson, and Paul Breslin have produced useful studies on the subject as well. As both a poet and a critic, however, I feel a continued urgency regarding the vexed notion of the self, and in what follows I can only gesture to some of my varied reasons for this feeling.

An understanding of the self is dialectical by definition, but that dialectic becomes particularly poignant when cast into any contemporary literary discourse. From the mythopoeic negations of the deep imagists to the radical disjunctions of the language poets—in both these groups' attitudes toward the self, we can find no better proof of Charles Newman's assertion in *The Post-Modern Aura*, that "an inflationary culture, because its overlapping realities are not only proliferating but cancelling each other out, tends to polarize theories as it recirculates them." Recognizable period styles and the poets in whose work they can be seen most clearly (and these are not always the best poets of a given period) provide the critic with the material needed to make such generalizations concrete. Likewise, "poetry wars," though they often leave a bad taste in a reader's mouth, seem to be an inescapable feature of the modern literary landscape. But reified styles and controversies of poets (which sometimes truly emerge from poetic practices and sometimes are imposed by critics and literary historians) not only polarize and recirculate theories of poetry but obscure alternative lines of inquiry in a given historical period.

Why is this so? Surely what Fredric Jameson calls "the cultural logic of late capitalism" has much to do with this situation, and here I will have recourse to Jameson's persuasive analysis of postmodern culture. I could also cite the unprecedented abutments of literary theory upon poetic practice, as seen, for example, in the multifaceted project of the language poets, and the tendency to simultaneously broaden and subvert the traditional domain of the lyric poem through various dissolutions of genre and work into "text." As the questions "What is a poet?" and "What is a poem?" become increasingly difficult to answer, in recent years we also have witnessed the deaths of a number of figures who, regardless of their still contested legacies, were models of poetic *integrity* in all the senses of that word: among others I have George Oppen and Robert Duncan in mind. The closure that the deaths of great poets lend to this moment, the self-conscious theoretical articulations of postmodem literary practices, and the arrival of new and diverse talents, combine to produce a threshold effect. It is on this threshold that I wish to ponder the fate of the "lyric I" and its equally problematic concomitant notion, the poetic voice.

According to Jameson in *Postmodernism*, one of the distinctions between the modern and the postmodern can be observed in "the dynamics of cultural pathology," which "can be characterized as one in which the alienation of the subject is displaced by the fragmentation of the subject." Developing this distinction, Jameson states: "As for expression and feeling or emotions, the liberation, in contemporary society, from the older *anomie* of the centred subject may also mean, not merely a liberation from anxiety, but a liberation from every other kind of feeling as well, since there is no longer a self present to do the feeling. This is not to say that the cultural products of the postmodern era are utterly devoid of feeling, but rather that such feelings—which it may be better and more accurate to call 'intensities'—are now free-floating and impersonal, and tend to be dominated by a peculiar kind of euphoria." Putting aside the often misleading question of periodization, this analysis can prove quite helpful in trying to understand some recent changes in what could be called lyric poetry's self-regard. At the same time, however, Jameson's analysis should be applied with caution: it could easily foster that polarization of theory which Newman sees as endemic to contemporary culture. Besides, major artists of whatever period break all the rules.

With this in mind, consider W. S. Merwin's brief poem "The Room," from *The Lice* (1967):

> I think all this is somewhere in myself
> The cold room unlit before dawn
> Containing a stillness such as attends death
> And from a corner the sounds of a small bird trying
> From time to time to fly a few beats in the dark
> You would say it was dying it is immortal.

The room or interior space which Merwin depicts in this poem by now is very familiar to readers of the deep image poetry which flourished from the mid sixties to the mid seventies. I take the poem's "I" and "you" to be aspects of the self; a viable relation between the self and the exterior world could not be considered even a remote possibility. What matters, what is at stake, is self-regard. Will the interior life die to itself? Will the alienation which prevails in the self's relation to the world likewise prevail within? The lyric "I" asserts the immortality of the interior: symbolically the bird of the soul will continue to fly despite the dark. The "you," the self at its most hopeless, speaks for negation, death, oblivion. The poem, as a representation of the self's inner space, thus becomes the site of a debate which, although it cannot be resolved, signifies the importance of the status of the self to itself. Although the self obviously is not a unified entity, it wishes to preserve its autonomy within its own hermetic place—the place where the voice can speak and, tautologically, maintain the place of the poem. As Merwin says in "Teachers," from *The Carrier of Ladders* (1970), "what I live for I can seldom believe in / who I love I cannot go to /

what I hope is always divided."

The best poetry of this style and sensibility can be regarded as a struggle in which the self, already driven into the depths of post-romantic interiority, attempts to determine the value of its integrity and autonomy. Obsessed with doubts, the lyric I enacts a series of mythopoeic rituals, endlessly rehearsing its annihilation and secretly relishing the agonizing possibility of its total absence and the poetic silence that would ensue. No poet has understood this more clearly than Mark Strand, which may account for the fact that of all the poets writing in this frequently criticized mode, he has been singled out for some of the harshest attacks. But despite Strand's occasional failure to maintain his necessary balance between melodrama and irony, his phantasmagoric play of absence and presence reveals as much about the contemporary self as any other poet of any style in recent years. Here is "The Remains," from his best book, *Darker* (1970):

> I empty myself of the names of others. I empty my pockets.
> I empty my shoes and leave them beside the road.
> At night I turn back the clocks;
> I open the family album and look at myself as a boy.
>
> What good does it do? The hours have done their job.
> I say my own name. I say goodbye.
> The words follow each other downwind.
> I love my wife but send her away.
>
> My parents rise out of their thrones
> into the milky rooms of clouds.
> Time tells me what I am. I change and I am the same.
> I empty myself of my life and my life remains.

In Jameson's terms, this might be considered a poem of modern anomie rather than of postmodern euphoria, though the exhilaration of masochistic nostalgia that runs through the text surely is familiar to all contemporary readers. Against Paul Breslin, in his book *The Psycho-Political Muse*, who sees Jung behind most of the deep imagists, this is an altogether Freudian poem: Strand's memorializing gestures of loss denote the childish repetition compulsion which, when observed by Freud, led him, in his most harrowing work, beyond the pleasure principle. It is out of this ritualized renunciation of pleasure ("I love my wife but send her away") and self-inflicted doubt ("How can I sing?") that the self is maintained and the poem is uttered. The I and the poem know themselves to exist through an act of negation that must be endlessly repeated. As Strand ironically concludes the litany called "Giving Myself Up": "I give up. I give up. / And you will have none of it because already I am beginning / again without anything."

If the morbid repetition compulsion of poets like Strand and Merwin, this ritualized play of annihilation, has fallen out of fashion in the last few years, then another, supposedly more extreme assault on the self has taken its place. As we have seen, the deep imagist attitude toward the self is ambivalent: the poem is a mythopoeic, interior space in which the guilty pleasure of annihilation is set against the equally guilty desire for what Strand calls "keeping things whole." Following Jameson, this is a kind of late-modern angst: Kafka without the fecundity of his parables, Beckett without his tenacity and breadth. Instead, we have the oddly poignant lyric purity of the self forever on the brink. Gleefully push the self over the brink and the result is language poetry. For as poststructuralsm tells us, the abyss has little to do with darkness and silence: the abyss is filled with words. When the postmodern self shatters into fragments, each fragment writes on and on.

The language poets represent a break from or refusal of the linguistic, philosophical, and political assumptions that largely determined other styles of recent poetry. Their lineage consists of writers who cast the integrity of the self into doubt by questioning referentiality and emphasizing the materiality of language: Stein, Zukofsky, Creeley, Spicer, the Ashbery of *The Tennis Court Oath*. At the same time, they have bolstered their work with references to Marx, Wittgenstein, the Russian Formalists, and the poststructuralists, marking them as the only group of contemporary poets willing to engage in extensive theorizing. Indeed, part of the program of the language poets has been a challenge to traditional distinctions between verse and prose, literature and philosophy, aesthetics and politics. And yet, despite these well-documented characteristics, I would argue that the assault on the self, though it is now conducted through linguistic defarniliarization rather than mythic negation, represents an ideological constant in the poetry of our time. But the real irony regarding language poetry is that the self, despite the massive linguistic displacements it undergoes, proves less subject to fragmentation than has been thought. Charles Bernstein may believe that "It's a mistake . . . to posit the self as the primary organizing feature of writing," but in the most intriguing texts by language poets—as with the work of Strand and Merwin—the self is a flickering presence of compelling power. However divided or dispersed, it continues its lyric utterance, its language of desire.

Bernstein's own poetry provides a convenient example. In his essay on language poetry, Jerome McGann cites Bernstein's "For Love Has Such a Spirit That If It Is Portrayed It Dies" as a "Shelleyan performance" despite its shifting "forms of order" and its essentially "antinarrative" stance. The first part of the poem is indeed produced under conditions of great semantic and grammatical dispersion, so that the direct expression of personal feelings which one expects of the lyric I of the traditional love poem is continually thwarted:

> Aims departing after one another
> & you just steps away, listening,
> listless. Alright, always—riches
> of that uncomplicated promise. Who—what—.
> That this reassurance (announcement)
> & terribly prompted—almost,
> although. Although censorious and even more
> careless. Lyrical mysticism—harbor, departing
> windows. For love I would—deft equator.

Here certain phrases associated with love ("you just steps away," "that uncomplicated promise," "lyrical mysticism") are interrupted or broken off before the emotion can be fully portrayed: surely a subversion of the self as the primary organizing feature of the poem. Even Creeley, whom Bernstein admires, is implicitly criticized for his plain expression of feeling by the phrase "For love I would—deft equator," a disruption of the first lines of Creeley's "The Warning" ("For love—I would / split open your head").

But what makes this poem more than a display of postmodern techniques is the way that the lyric I reasserts itself about halfway through the text. Language poets admire Jack Spicer for the ghostly voices which disturb personal utterance in many of his books. In Bernstein's poem, just the opposite occurs, as out of the cacophony a relatively stable voice begins to speak, and quite movingly at that:

> This darkness, how richer than a moat it lies. And
> my love, who takes my hand, now, to watch all this
> pass by, has only care, she and I. We deceive
> ourselves in this matter because we are in
> the habit of thinking the leaves will fall or
> that there are few ways of breaking the circuit.
> How much the stronger we would have been had
> not—but it is something when one is lonely
> and miserable to imagine history on your side. On
> the stoop, by the door ledge, we stand here, coffee
> in hand.

The bittersweet feeling of regret in these lines (reminiscent of Ashbery at his most humane), the sheer wistfulness of that one broken sentence, while they do not altogether negate the language poets' programmatic repudiation of the self, certainly cast their attitude in a more ambiguous light. It is this ambiguity toward the self, the distrust of the I and its voice and the continued necessity of coherent lyric utterance, that connects language writing with other, less drastically postmodern styles of contemporary poetry.

The literary and philosophical traditions from which language poetry emerges have radically interrogated the unified, autonomous individual subject, leading, as in language poetry itself, to its almost total dissolution in the more abstract play of social and discursive forces. But to abandon the notion of the individual is indefensible, and hardly on poetic grounds alone. As Paul Smith observes in *Discerning the Subject*, his ambitious study of the subject in recent theory: "What is at stake here is a sense of how and under what conditions subject/individuals simultaneously exist within and make purposive intervention into social formations. Such intervention can and does take place, actively or passively, through single people or collectives, privately and publicly. It can take the form of a refusal as much as an intervention; it can be in the service of conservatism as much as of disruption. It may well call upon an experience of class; but more generally it calls upon the subject/individual's history."

In a sense, what we are debating when we speak of the status of the self in poetry is nothing other than the social and political responsibility of the poet. Poets with very different styles and attitudes toward language have criticized the notion of the autonomous individual because of its capitulation to and support of the status quo. In Merwin's "The Old Room," for instance, the repeated phrase "It is not me," declared in various murky and insidious public circumstances, indicates how desperate the poet's desire can be to dissociate the self from what is understood to be the destructive network of social and political relations in which it must always participate:

> there is a poll at the corner I am not to go in
> but I can look in the drugstore window
> where the numbers of the dead change all night on the wall
> what if I vote *It is not me* will they revive
> I go in my father has voted for me
> I say no I will vote in my own name
> I vote and the number leaps again on the wall

For Bernstein, however, as he explains in his essay "Writing and Method," even the most experimental writing in the twentieth century (stream-of-consciousness, surrealism, expressionism, etc.), out of which a poem like "The Old Room" comes, "leaves the reader as sealed-off from the self enacted within it as conventional writ ing does from the world pictured within it. The experience is of a self bound off from me in its autonomy, enclosed in its self-sufficiency." As we have seen, the final step after such frustration is the systematic dismantling of coherent linguistic order as predicated upon the principle of the speaking subject (sealed-off or not, since, as Bernstein rather facilely says in "The Dollar Value of Poetry," "Caesar himself is the patron of our grammar books.") But the political if not poetic efficacy of this stance, like that of the deep imagists, is dubious, as the potential for what Smith calls "intervention" is lost to the poem. Instead, the poem, in its antagonism to the self, becomes an ironic reification of the very forces it yearns to overthrow. Again we encounter the paradigm of "literature against itself" which Gerald Graff identified many years ago. As Graff argues, "The more violently the arts overturn objective consciousness, the represertational view of art, and the common language, the more surely do they guarantee their marginality and harmlessness—a condition which, in turn, inspires renewed artistic attempts to overturn objective consciousness, representation, and common language."

The distinction—and it is an important one—that can be made finally regarding the self in the two types of poetry before us is that while the deep imagists ritualistically critique the unified subject (or what Graff calls "objective consciousness"), seeking to undo it through a kind of negative expressivity, the language poets not only at tempt to decenter or fragment the subject but also try to undermine the notion of expressivity itself. Expressivity, however, can never be completely dispersed; it is inextricably bound to all poetic utterance. (The silence of a poet too is expressive, perhaps even strategic, as in the case of George Oppen.)

Fredric Jameson's notorious analysis of Bob Perelman's "China" as a kind of euphoric, schizophrenic disjunction participating in the cultural dominant of postmodernism therefore makes a good deal a sense, as long as one recognizes that linguistic strategies of disjunction which attempt to undo the I are always marked as just that: strategies. The poet as a practitioner of verbal deformation, as a producer of depersonalized utterance, founders on the enduring shoals of selfhood. Expressivity cannot be avoided, and expression always bears at least the trace of the I. As Barrett Watten says in his poem "Mode Z":

> Prove to me now that you have finally undermined
> your heroes. In fits of distraction the walls cover

themselves with portraits. Types are not men. Admit
that your studies are over. Limit yourself to your
memoirs. Identity is only natural. Now become
the person in your life. Start writing autobiography.

However ironically these sharply delivered lines are meant, Watten
is right: at least in the kingdom of poetry, identity is only natural.

II

The Avant-Garde

I will now pursue my line of argument in a somewhat different
direction, paying particular attention to the language poets in their role
of a literary avant-garde. Let us keep in mind that the double nature of
the avant-garde has always been troublesome. The category implies
both formal experimentation that would secure artistic autonomy, and
revolutionary gestures that would make artists into a social and even
political vanguard. At the same time, avant-gardes are notorious for
their publicizing and marketing strategies, leading critics to suspect
that avant-gardes are an indispensable component of the cultural
superstructure of bourgeois society. "The genuine art of bourgeois society can only be anti-bourgeois," says Renato Poggioli in his classic
Theory of the Avant-Garde. But he also observes that "Avant-garde art ...
cannot help paying involuntary homage to democratic and liberal-
bourgeois society in the very act of proclaiming itself antidemocratic
and antibourgeois; nor does it realize that it expresses the evolutionary
and progressive principle of that social order in the very act of abandoning itself to the opposite chimeras of involution and revolution."

Poggioli's analysis has been extended in Charles Newman's *The
Post-Modern Aura*. Newman argues that the original dialectical relationship between avant-garde and bourgeoisie has become even more
complicated due to what is by now the long-standing cultural hege-
mony of modernism. But the success of this "First Revolution" comes
to us now through a "Second Revolution," "the revolution in pedagogy

and criticism which interpreted, canonized and capitalized the Modernist industry, making 'the contemporary' the indubitable cultural reference point." To a great extent, it is this Second Revolution which constitutes postmodernism. As Newman would have it, "while the activity of interpretation, codification and certification are routinely scorned, it is nevertheless incorporated with begrudging *elan* into the Post-Modern aesthetic."

It is my assumption that language poetry partakes of this version of the postmodern aesthetic, though its *elan* may hardly be begrudging at all. Part of the program of the language poets has been an invigorating challenge to traditional distinctions between verse and prose, literature and philosophy, aesthetics and politics, as well as to the institutions that maintain such distinctions. But as Poggioli wryly notes, "even the avant-garde has to live and work in the present, accept compromises and adjustments, reconcile itself with the official culture of the times, and collaborate with at least some part of the public." That "part of the public" toward which writers in our day gravitate is, of course, academia. In a paradoxically self-promoting move, the language poets have lambasted the academy, which has been all too eager to lionize them and admit some of them into its ranks. Such is the nature of today's avant-gardes in relation to the university: as Raymond Williams observes in his analysis of emergent practices in relation to the dominant culture, "The alternative, especially in areas that impinge on significant areas of the dominant, is often seen as oppositional and, by pressure, often converted to it." Language poetry, as an emergent writing practice, certainly offers an alternative to dominant modes, and often presents itself as oppositional. Whether this is truly the case remains to be seen, but I suspect that for all its subversive claims, language poetry is gradually (and happily) being absorbed by the university, the dominant institution which mediates nearly all literary activity in the latter part of our century.

Perhaps what is ultimately a more serious but still related charge is that the theoretical work of the language poets is more lively and thought-provoking than their actual poems, which tend to be formulaic and constituted of a fairly predictable set of gestures—though perhaps no more predictable than any other period style in the history of verse. Tom Beckett raises this issue in an interview with Charles Bernstein, referring generally to the contributors to the journal $L=A=N=G=U=A=G=E$ as well as to Bernstein in particular. Bernstein replies by arguing that "There is an annoying bait in this type of disassociative discrimination insofar as it's fueled by a valorization of the Poet who only writes Poetry (in the narrower sense of the verse tradition), since it is out of fear of this type of criticism, of being typed as a theoretician in mutual exclusion to being a Poet, that I think causes many poets to retreat from expressing themselves in modes other than verse, as if to include non-'poetic' subject matter or diction in one's writing taints the purity of the project. This view you suggest seems primarily a negation of the whole activity, *both,* perhaps out of a sense that it punctures the privileged domain of poetic discourse, and challenges the self-imposed limits of what the vocabulary and style of poetry are. So I would think the person who makes this point doesn't know *where* to find the poetry. Whatever 'critical' writing I've done makes sense primarily in terms of the 'poetry', is one and the same project."

In this passage we can see both the strengths and the weaknesses of the position which Bernstein represents. Bernstein is right to attack the anti-intellectual prejudice against poets theorizing about their poetry, and one has only to reflect upon the history of English poetry to realize how many major poets produced essential critical statements as well. His insistence that dominant poetic conventions need not restrict the style or subject of the poem is also well-taken; likewise, we should honor his more personal claim that "It is inconceivable that what you are calling the theoretical essays could have developed without an active poetic practice." But to what extent does this unity or reciprocity of poetry and theory affect our actual encounter with the poem? In what ways does the poem, without its theoretical corollaries, call upon us to read differently—and are we willing to be taught new ways of reading this particular poem?

It would appear that Bernstein has not been careful enough in his discussion of the relationship between poetics and poetry, between theory and practice. This is understandable: for the poet-critic like Bernstein (and many of the other language poets), the two activities inevitably come to be regarded as part of a single project (though other poets take the route of writing a "poetics" through their practice alone). But for the reader, who may not be a critic or a poet, the relationship of the poem to its theoretical justification is secondary at best; theory is, as I just said, only a corollary to practice. The reader puts poetry to the test, and as Zukofsky tells us, "The test of poetry is the range of pleasure it affords as sight, sound, and intellection. This is its purpose as art." Language poetry, like all avant-garde writing, challenges the conventional means through which poetic pleasure is produced, variously manipulating the techniques of sight, sound, and intellection which constitute the poem. Through such manipulation, the boundaries of the poem could presumably be expanded indefinitely, accommodating whatever forms the avant-garde writer achieves: as Wallace Stevens says, "All poetry is experimental poetry." Some experiments, however, are not as successful as others, regardless of how meticulously their procedures are described. But such judgments depend in turn on the reason that the experiments were conducted in the first place.

What language writing as a totalizing project asks of us, in effect, is a reevaluation of the notion of literary pleasure. The modernist insistence on the difficulty of readerly pleasure appears relatively tame in the face of much of the language poets' work. In opposition to the modernism of a Zukofsky or a Stevens, language poetry no longer assumes that the Supreme Fiction must give "pleasure" at all, since "pleasure" is the dominant motivation and goal in the consumer society of late capitalism. As Jerome McGann observes, language poetry "does not propose for its immediate object pleasure, as Coleridge once said all poetry does. Its immediate objects are the illusions of pleasure." In that most language poets are left-wing post-structuralists, this challenge makes perfect sense: after all, political conservatives have no qualms about referentiality, and certainly have no desire to question the unity of the (bourgeois) subject. These issues concern the language poets to such a great extent because they represent the most vulnerable of dominant cultural assumptions about the production and consumption of literature in a postmodern capitalist society. If poetry continues to be read for pleasure, and if that pleasure is to endure through the most rigorous engagement with pressing historical circumstances, then the language poets are right to exploit these concerns in order to reorient our political experience of poetic gratification. But as Fredric Jameson says, if a specific pleasure "is to become genuinely political" then it "must always in one way or another also be able to stand as a figure for the transformation of social relations as a whole." In other words, what is at issue here is language poetry's utopian propensity.

Reading, as I have implied, is different from writing insofar as the reading self in its ineluctable search for meaning and pleasure (or perhaps meaning *as* pleasure) longs to encounter an other which it can gradually know in the contours of the other's alternative subjectivity. In order for a work of literature to be more than a consumable commodity ("culinary" literature, as Hans Robert Jauss puts it), it must undermine reader expectations. There is no better way to accomplish this than to thwart that search for the subjectivity of an other by defamiliarizing the referent and continually repositioning the voices of the text. But the risk involved in this strategy may be just as serious as that involved in simply following the accepted conventions of a given genre: whereas in the latter case, the text may be consumed as a mere entertainment, in the former case, the text may be rejected as offering too little that gratifies the reader's desire to encounter an alternative subjectivity. Whether the writer's goal regarding his or her audience is social transformation or formal accomplishment (and of course, these are not mutually exclusive), endless defamiliarization may prove as ineffectual as strict adherence to the standards of a generic status quo.

Language poets succeed when they resist the temptation to push their avant-garde strategies to the limit. We usually think of groundbreaking literature as extremist in some dimension, but in this case, the formal extremism of the writing is such that the work frequently is hurled back on itself, inadvertently producing an obscurantism that goes against the express intentions of the writer. In "Disappearance of the Word, Appearance of the World," one of the most important (and explicitly Marxist) documents of the movement, Ron Silliman explains that "What happens when a language moves toward and passes into a capitalist stage of development is an anaesthetic transformation of the perceived tangibility of the word, with corresponding increases in its expository, descriptive and narrative capacities, preconditions for the invention of 'realism', the illusion of reality in capitalist thought. These developments are tied directly to the function of reference in language, which under capitalism is transformed, narrowed into referentiality." For Silliman, the politically engaged writer attempts to reverse this "anaesthetic transformation" by "placing the issue of language, the repressed signifier, at the center of the program" and "placing the program into the context of conscious class struggle."

The irony here is that Silliman's own writing focuses on the previously repressed signifier to such an extent that its expository, descriptive, and narrative capacities are almost totally lost. In *Tjanting*, his book-length prose work, a transformation takes places that is every bit as "anaesthetic" as that which ostensibly occurs to language in a "capitalist stage of development." What begins as an interesting experiment in self-deconstructing personal narrative becomes an increasingly disjointed barrage of sentences: "My shadow on the off-white wall is writing. Slippery elm throat lozenge. Cat chooses to sit atop flat old brown paper bag. Fine pharmaceuticals since blah blah. Utter filth verb noun someone to clean up mouse parts cat puke. His eyes burnd right into his skull smell of tobacco in hair & shirt. Modular stool drop. By now familiar territory. Need to make do. Prisms' little rainbows on wall till clouds loom up. Nothing to do with the previous thing. Active ingredients." Granted, there is a certain exuberance here, a delight in the heterogeneity of contemporary discourse. And Marjorie Perloff is right to note, in her comparison of a passage from *Tjanting* to a sentimental reminiscence in a poem by Galway Kinnell, that Silliman's work usefully counters an obsessive concern with the uniqueness of personal experience with a more self-conscious "familiarity with literary codes" instead. But what Perloff does not note is that while readers are at first sensitized to the play of the signifier in *Tjanting*, they gradually succumb to the obsessive sameness of the technique. Although many of Silliman's sentences could be identified as minute descriptions of the author's day-to-day existence, their random intermingling with sentences based on a wide variety of other codes finally results in the work's numbing style. The utopian murmur of language celebrated by such theorists as Michel Foucault turns out to be an interminable, affectless chat.

This is not to single out Silliman for harsh criticism. Like most of the writers identified with language poetry, he combines leftist ideology, poststructuralist theory, and an avant-garde posture in a simultaneous effort to politicize art and aestheticize politics. The result is not a new, alternative notion of "realism," as is claimed for these writers' work (often by and in support of each other), but a fin-de-siecle style as rarefied as that of any Pre-Raphaelite or Symbolist. Late nineteenth-century aestheticism gives us an ecstatically cloying literature in which spirit and flesh, death and beauty, are proven to be one and the same. Late twentieth-century aestheticism gives us a literature in which, all such binary oppositions having been deconstructed, language finally absorbs and nullifies reality while claiming to enact it and give it new life.

The methods as well as the theoretical underpinning of language poetry cannot be dismissed, but perhaps the time has come to see past both the self-promotion and the oppositional gestures of this latest avant-garde. Indeed, perhaps the time has come to question the efficacy of avant-gardism in itself, though it may also be true that the avant-garde, like the poor, will always be with us, and for the same reasons.

In speaking of the role played by groups of relatively young or unknown writers "with certain affinities or regional sympathies between them," T. S. Eliot tells us that "Such groups frequently bind themselves together by formulating a set of principles or rules, to which usually nobody adheres; in course of time the group disintegrates, the feebler members vanish, and the stronger ones develop more individual styles. But the group, and the group anthology, serve a useful purpose: young poets do not ordinarily get, and indeed are better without, much attention from the general public, but they need the support and criticism of each other, and of a few other people."

The language poets are no longer young; they have produced a number of group anthologies (such as Silliman's *In the American Tree* and Douglas Messerli's *"Language" Poetries*); and at this point the strongest among them have indeed developed more individual styles. These writers would best be served through focusing critical attention on them as individuals, still keeping in mind the principles and affinities which led to the formation of their group identity and reputation.

I am aware that in calling for greater scrutiny of the work through the lens of the individual writer, I am violating an article of faith shared by post-structuralist theorists and the language poets themselves: that criticism should question, if not explode, what was once, in Foucault's words, "the solid and fundamental unit of the author and the work." The taboo against the authorial self as a fundamental unit of criticism has, in the case of the language poets, successfully concentrated attention instead on the political principles of an alternative literary collectivity and on the formal principles of an alternative notion of poetic language. I use the term "alternative" for I cannot use the term "oppositional." The ways in which these principles of language poetry operate in a number of increasingly mature and distinct (though still related) personal styles remain to be explored.

THE ACADEMY,
THE AVANT-GARDE,
AND THE POET-CRITIC:
HISTORICAL OBSERVATIONS,
HERMENEUTICAL SPECULATIONS

Despite my title, I begin with neither history nor hermeneutics, but with autobiography. It is the fall of 1974 in Binghamton, New York, and I am a senior preparing to apply to graduate school. As an English major, I have concentrated in both literature and creative writing, and though I briefly consider the MFA, I quickly decide in favor of doctoral programs in literature. From now on, my poetry will have to take care of itself.

In retrospect, it was not merely my critical bent that led me to this decision, since my poetry continued to grow in intellectual ambition and affective power not only the more I read literature, but also the more I read literary criticism and theory as well. My decision was also a matter of poetic affinities: unlike most of my creative writing instructors, who preferred either Sylvia Plath or Robert Bly, I was one of those young poets in the sixties and seventies who schlepped around Donald Allen's *New American Poetry* as if it were Holy Writ. That anthology, including the "Statements on Poetics" section, probably influenced my thinking about poetry more than other book, and at an age when I was most susceptible to such influence. But despite my enthusiasm for the avant-garde poets of Black Mountain, the San Francisco Renaissance, and the New York School, the environment in which I read them, wrote about them, and argued for their importance was, and still is, thoroughly academic.

Five years later, at Emory, I write a Marxist-inflected dissertation on modalities of poetic interiority and exteriority from Yeats to Jack

Spicer, with stops at Pound, Williams, Olson Oppen, and Duncan. Meanwhile the rejection slips keep piling up: my poetry is too "abstract" or "intellectual" for the mainstream literary magazines, but too dependent upon Romantic notions of prophetic voice and subjective authority for the avant-garde scene, which is increasingly dominated by tendencies we have since come to identify with language writing. By the early eighties, my critical essays are appearing with some regularity in academic journals. It takes quite a while for my poetry to catch up, but eventually it too makes its way into print, first in university-sponsored literary magazines, and then through a university press.

Although I'm hesitant to put myself forward in this fashion, I feel that my experience may serve as a useful example of the formation of the poet-critic in a period when the academy (or to be precise, the English Department) has become such a magnetic literary institution that, to a greater or lesser extent, it mediates nearly all significant poetic transactions that take place in American culture. In speaking of the poet-critic, I have in mind Michel Foucault's analysis of what he calls the "author function" in his haunting essay "What Is an Author?" For Foucault, the author function "does not develop spontaneously as the attribution of a discourse to an individual. It is, rather, the result of a complex operation which constructs a certain rational being that we call 'author'. . . . these aspects of an individual which we designate as making him an author are only a projection, in more or less psychologizing terms, of the operations that we force texts to undergo, the connections that we make, the traits that we establish as pertinent, the continuities that we recognize, or the exclusions that we practice. All these operations vary according to periods and types of discourse. We do not construct a 'philosophical author' as we do a 'poet' just as, in the eighteenth century, one did not construct a novelist as we do today." Thus, through a gradual sequence of connections, continuities, traits, and exclusions, a set of texts, duly "psychologized" and associated with the proper name "Norman Finkelstein," can be invested (in a decidedly minor fashion) with the author function termed "poet-critic."

So let us turn our attention to some of those connections, continuities, traits and exclusions through which the poet-critic has come into being as an identifiable author function, characterizing, as for Foucault such a figure always does, "the mode of existence, circulation, and functioning of certain discourses within a society." I have already invoked the academy as a mediating institution for almost all contemporary poetic transactions. It is here that poetry is read, studied, debated, and judged; it is here, given the growth and popularity of creative writing programs, that much of it is written; and it is here, through journals housed in English departments and through university presses, that much of it is published, especially given the seriously reduced commitment to poetry of commercial publishing houses. As Ron Silliman puts it in his essay "Canons and Institutions: New Hope for the Disappeared," "the university is the 500 pound gorilla at the party of poets." But as such studies as Gerald Graff's *Professing Literature* demonstrate, university English departments, from their inception, have been constituted not through any consensus regarding methods, goals, or ideology, but through "a series of conflicts that have tended to be masked by their very failure to find visible institutional expression." These conflicts include the current one between creative writing and literary theory, which were both new kids on the institutional block not so long ago. I take it for a good sign, however painful, that in recent years this particular conflict, like others in the field, has been increasingly visible. At least some theorists and creative writers have come to share in the belief that we are mutually impoverished when we ignore or deny the insight into the imaginative process that only reflective theory can provide, and conversely, that our theoretical understanding of culture can develop only through contact with new acts of the imagination.

This may be especially true in regard to poetry, which remains, in George Oppen's deceptively simple phrase, "a test of truth." Arguably, poetry is not only that mode of literary discourse that can enact the most spontaneous movements of individual experience with the greatest linguistic concentration, but historically, it has rigorously tested that experience against the objective demands of form. And this is why poets themselves have tended to reflect or theorize upon their activity. From the Renaissance through the period of high modernism, the most important critical statements on poetry were authored by poets, usually attempting to distinguish their practices from older poetic modes or competing discourses, such as those of religion, history, philosophy or positive science. The institutionalization of literary studies in the academy which began in the nineteenth century tended to reify the distinction between writing as original act and writing as commentary, with the latter given precedence in the modern formation of the discipline. Nevertheless, poets have played an important role in the study of literature on American campuses for a very long time, though the critical and educational philosophies that they have represented have surely changed. Graff notes that "Harvard virtually invented the generalist-professor before the Civil War when it engaged Henry Wadsworth Longfellow and later James Russell Lowell to teach Dante and other modern European writers, and Lowell became famous for the casual, impressionistic style of teaching." Closer to our time, and more directly influential on the current situation, we have the New Critics, who are largely responsible for the shift from literary history to close reading and textual explication that took place from the late thirties through the fifties. After surveying the academic situations of members this group up through the early forties, Graff observes that "many of the first critics to achieve a foothold in the university did so on the strength of their poetry rather than their criticism. It is worth pondering the probability that the critical movement would not have succeeded had it not been tied to creative writing, from which it was soon to part company."

Pondering just this probability in *From Outlaw to Classic: Canons In American Poetry,* Alan Golding makes a strong case for the New Critics as highly self-conscious "poet-professors" whose significance "lies in their effort to import the role of the evaluative poet-critic into the academy. They wanted both to maintain evaluation as the central critical function of the amateur, nonacademic man of letters and also to give that function a professional power base. . . . it was through the academy that they could most effectively institutionalize and gain an audience for the acts of evaluation that had historically been the preserve of public criticism." For Golding, the New Critics' sustained argument for the canonic status of modernist poetry (represented first and foremost by T. S. Eliot) stemmed in part from their own poetic practice, as well as the fact that poets "have traditionally felt themselves responsible for evaluation, especially of contemporary literature." The poet-professors of the New Criticism thus entered (and transformed) English departments with a new method (close reading), a new canon (modernism and its antecedents), and a new mission (the evaluation of literature). From the overt agrarian conservatism of *I'll Take My Stand*, the New Critics made what Graff describes as "a concerted move" in the early forties to establish their beliefs and practices at the center of literary studies through teaching positions, the editing of such journals as *Kenyon Review, Sewanee Review,* and the *Southern Review,* and per-haps above all, through the extraordinarily successful textbook *Understanding Poetry.*

But as many chroniclers of the profession now inform us, the New Critical agenda for the academy could not be fully sustained. While the method of close reading came to dominate the English classroom and the difficult narrative of modernism came to dominate accounts of the poetic canon, the task of evaluation fell away—except, ironically, in creative writing programs, where evaluation of student work by instructors and fellow students remains a fundamental activity, but where the challenge of modernist aesthetics—and of modernist *critique*—rarely been met. Since the dramatic expansion of creative writing programs of the sixties and seventies, most poets in the academy see themselves as practitioners of a literary craft, and it is on the basis of craftsmanship of a limited sort that creative writing students tend to be evaluated. But for over ten years, the ideology of this craftsmanship, the verbal gestures and tonal values associated with what Charles Altieri calls the "scenic mode" or Marjorie Perloff more recently names a poetic of "strenuous authenticity," has been thoroughly, often glee-fully deconstructed by critics with allegiance to the defamiliarizing rig-ors of modernism. The evaluative academic critic has returned, every bit as formidable as his or her New Critical predecessor.

But it is not only the critics, whose methods have grown increas-ingly sophisticated and whose theorized attitudes toward writing more rarefied, who have led the charge against the workshop poem. Since the seventies, avant-garde poets, experimentalists who have delved deeply into theory, have also been among the most vocal opponents of that period style which we now associate with most creative writing programs of the sixties through the eighties, with its stable voice, conversational tone, transparently referential discourse, and hyptrophied valorization of individual memory and affect. By avant-garde poets, I refer primarily but not exclusively to the language writers, taken less as a specific group of authors than as a larger body that shares what Bob Perelman calls "a generalizable set of concerns." In *The Marginalization of Poetry: Language Writing and Literary History,* Perelman acknowledges language writers' use of structuralist and post-structuralist theory while also emphasizing their relation to "writing practices closely informed by the modernists, especially Stein, and the Objectivists, especially Zukofsky, and by Black Mountain, Beat, and New York School poetry. Thus—to be schematic about it—language writing occupies a middle territory bounded on the one side by poetry as it is currently instituted and on the other by theory." Perelman's position in this book is quite revealing: to a greater extent than any of the other language poets, he attempts self-reflexively to delineate the aesthetic and sociohistorical status of what began as an avant-garde formation and a set of writing practices in which he himself is a crucial participant. At the same time, for all his self-reflexive play and generically blurred exposition, Perelman inevitably assumes the role of the engaged poet-professor, resembling, at least from a sociohistorical perspective, the combative New Critics who came before him. Analyzing, evaluating, and advocating contemporary poetry with the strongest affinities to his own, Perelman argues that what truly distinguishes language writing from both the discourse of theory and the discourse of mainstream, workshop-bred poetry is its "foregrounding writing as an active process."

But that is hardly the only factor that sets language writing apart from these discourses. As a movement, language writing first presents itself as an avant-garde through both historical filiation and alternative cultural formations (small presses and magazines, lectures and performances in galleries and clubs, etc.). An avant-garde traditionally opposes itself to such centralized power structures as the university, and indeed, early on, members of the original language group frequently attack what Charles Bernstein, in an essay in *Content's Dream,* calls "official verse culture," which he sees "housed and boarded by the academy." Soon, however, central figures in language writing are scrutinizing the question of avant-garde group identity and complicating their oppositional stance. Perelman contends that "internally, group structure is crucial: language writing is the activity that blurs the distinction between reader and writer, poet and critic; externally, group identity is disavowed: given the deep disinterest in poetics of identity, the creation of literary labels would hardly be desirable." And in the paper I cited above, Ron Silliman speaks of a "double-edged relationship of language poetry to the academy" which "foregrounds one of the primary features of that institution: the university is not a monolith, but rather an ensemble of competing and historically specific discourses and practices." Thus, for Silliman, "[i]t is even time to say out loud that there is nothing inherently wrong with being an academic poet" since the term occludes the poet's stand on such issues as "the role of the reader, the function of history, or the potential and responsibilities of the poem," and "inhibits those who use it from developing a fully nuanced reading of the very writing it seeks to identify."

Perelman's distinction between the "internal" and "external" group identification of language writing, and Silliman's "double-edged relationship of language poetry to the academy" point to a relatively recent shift in the dynamic of cultural institutionalization. In *The Theory-Death of the Avant-Garde*, Paul Mann argues that "[t]he death of the avant-garde is not its termination but its most productive, voluble, self-conscious, and lucrative stage. . . . this development has been brought about at the expense of a certain dialectical destabilization, perhaps even collapse: a theory-death. . . . The death of the avant-garde is its theory and the theory of the avant-garde is its death." If we apply this thesis to language writing (or more broadly, any postmodern avant-garde) and the academy, we see the inevitability, the necessity, of a richly unstable exchange "of what were once simply interiors and exteriors." In Mann's analysis, "[t]he avant-garde has in fact served, in most cases quite unwittingly, as an instrument for the incorporation of its own marginality. The avant-garde is the outside of the inside, the leading edge of the mainstream, and thus marginal in both senses: excluded and salient. The doubleness of this site, the existence of so curious and yet typical a phenomenon as a centralized margin, an internalized exterior, is another reason for the difficulty of discerning in the avant-garde a coherent ideological figure." This strikes me as a perfectly apt description of the projects of such poet-critics as Bernstein, Perelman, and Silliman, though there is nothing unwitting about the way their work serves as the instrument for the incorporation of their marginality. Thus, when critics of language writing, and when language writers themselves, functioning as their own critics, analyze the relation of this marginal group to the academic center, they take part in what Mann calls "the most fully articulated discourse of the technology of recuperation."

So where, then, does this leave poet-critics who wish to maintain the alternative, even oppositional status of formal experimentation? On the one hand, it may actually leave them better off. Given their academic berths (or at least the attention paid to them by academics), such figures automatically have a serious readership, and even if their work still isn't widely read, its polemical force is to be felt in that "ensemble of competing and historically specific discourses and practices" which we now understand the academy to be. On the other hand, it could be argued that when the technology of recuperation which Mann invokes is set into motion, the oppositional (or at least, defamiliarizing) power of a given writing practice is bound to be lost, resulting in another reified style to be imitated in creative writing classes: academic is the worst sense of the term.

In the belief that there is some truth to both of these alternatives, I am led back to a passage in T. S. Eliot's essay "What Is Minor Poetry?" Considering the way in which relatively young poets tend to gather together, Eliot notes that "Such groups frequently bind themselves together by formulating a set of principles or rules, to which usually nobody adheres; in course of time the group disintegrates, the feebler members vanish, and the stronger ones develop more individual styles." Eliot's formulation, with its emphasis on relative stylistic strength that results in a process of individuation (and, presumably, canonization), stands against the essay by Foucault that I cited above, for "What Is an Author" is an explicit attempt to deconstruct "the solid and fundamental unit of the author and the work"—an attempt that language writing, with its emphasis on shifting group identity and generic border crossings, strongly endorses. Can we then imagine a poet-critic for whom older discourses of authorial subjectivity, academic scholarship, and even canonic power still has relevance, who at the same time folds these traditional discourses into a self-consciously experimental project, theoretical in its orientation and oppositional in its stance? What would the writing of such a figure sound like? Perhaps it sounds something like this:

Names who are strangers out of bounds of the bound margin: I thought one way to write about a loved author would be to follow what trails he follows through words of others: what if these penciled single double and triple scorings arrows short phrases angry outbursts crosses cryptic ciphers sudden enthusiasms mysterious erasures have come to find you too, here again, now.

Round about the margin or edge of anything in a way that is close to the limit. A narrow margin. Slightly.

If water is margined-imagined by the tender grass.

Marginal. Belonging to the brink or margent.

The brink or brim of anything from telepathy to poetry.

A marginal growth of willow and water flag.

A feather on the edge of a bird's wing.

This is a passage from the preface of Susan Howe's "Melville's Marginalia," a work that appears in *The Nonconformist's Memorial*, a volume of poetry, but was originally intended for *The Birth-mark*, a book of literary criticism. One reason that Howe has emerged as an exemplary poet-critic is her commitment to writing a hermeneutics of the margin. By hermeneutics I mean a carrying-across, a movement between realms of discourse which radically interprets and inscribes one in terms of the other. In a certain respect, all of Howe's writing is marginalia, a writing that is, to use Mann's phrase, "excluded and salient." Just as her work challenges all the accepted discourses on gender, so too does it oppose accepted distinctions between scholarship and poetry, thus furthering the work of such precursors as Williams, Olson, Zukofsky, and Duncan. Indeed, Howe's relationship to traditional discursive categories is suffused with doubleness, producing, as it were, "a centralized margin." On the one hand, she maintains the utmost respect for her "loved authors" and their works, and much of her writing is concerned, either implicitly or explicitly, with the psychohistorical processes of individuation, canonization, and scriptural authority. On the other hand, because she understands that authors and works are caught up in the vicissitudes of these processes, her writing presents itself as a series of extreme enactments of them, exploded moments when the margins of reading and writing shift, transgressive textual interactions across the boundaries of time, genre, and personality. The techniques that Howe has developed, including strategic citation, fragmentation, collage, and echolalia, deconstruct the categories of both poetry and criticism as authority or full presence, reinscribing them as palpable absences, ghosts that hover over literature and history, as the figure of James Clarence Mangan hovers over Melville's *Bartleby*. What she says of Emily Dickinson—"Forcing, abbreviating, pushing, padding, subtracting, riddling, interrogating, rewriting, she pulled text from text"—can apply equally well to Howe herself.

In presenting Susan Howe in this context, I do not mean to imply that the kind of project in which she is engaged, with its radical redefinition of genre and pervasive interrogation of received notions of scriptural authority, is the only way in which contemporary poet-critics are posing a challenge to conventional views of academic and avant-garde poetry and criticism. Interestingly, it is in the name of some sort of poetic prophecy that these challenges are often made. I would like to mention a writer with a very different set of methods and assumptions than Howe, but one who also shakes our conventional views to the core: Allen Grossman. Contrary to many significant poet-critics today, Grossman argues in *The Sighted Singer* that "[i]f the poet has any function at the present time, it is to lay hold of this anxiety about true

presence, which is his inherited obligation, and to try to mediate a pro-
founder, more gratifying, more magnanimous, more joyous sense of
being toward persons in the world." Yet Grossman's astonishing book,
which is one of the most fully sustained attempts to describe the poet's
ancient claim to presence and renew it in a postmodern milieu, is also
one of the most theoretically wide-ranging and sophisticated works by
any poet in our time. "Theory," Grossman tells us, "is the deep dream
that precedes the description of a reality, the preconditions of which it
constructs. There is, in other words, a primitivity that underlies the
poetic motive of many writers in this age of theory." At a time when
most of us see the fascination with theory as a sign of literary exhaus-
tion, Grossman's is a particularly refreshing perspective—and one, I
think, at which only a poet could have arrived.

THE SERIAL POEM,
DICTATION,
AND THE STATUS OF THE LYRIC

The serial poem as conceived by such poets as Robert Duncan, Jack Spicer and Robin Blaser is a structure intended, in part, to combat what Spicer calls "the big lie of the personal" or what Charles Olson identifies as "the lyrical interference of the individual as ego." The lyric, of course, is the type of poem most closely associated with personal utterance, or, if you will, the expressivity of the subject. In the Vancouver Lectures, Spicer describes what he perceives to be the danger of the lyrical stance when he speaks in his admonitory fashion of "the poet being a beautiful machine which manufactured the current for itself, did everything for itself—almost a perpetual motion machine, of emotion, until the poet's heart broke, or was burned on the beach like Shelley's." In Spicer's view, Romantic lyricists in their pursuit of transcendence, the moment when the subject, through the expressive force of its utterance, achieves total, albeit unsustainable union with the Absolute, simply take too great a psychic risk.

It could be argued that Spicer is misrepresenting Romantic lyricism: such poets may appear at times to be appear perpetual [e]motion machines, but the Romantic crisis poems of Wordsworth, Coleridge, Shelley, and Keats actually involve the *memory* of transcendence which variously mediates the affective intensity of their utterances. Perhaps this misreading is due to Spicer having also been influenced by the modernist/objectivist aesthetic of Pound and Williams (and probably Olson too), a poetic which stresses conveying the immediacy of the object world. The objectivist stance holds an attraction for Spicer because, as he notes in *After Lorca*, objects do not believe the big lie of the personal. Unimpressed by the way the poet's personal life or desires creep into the poem, objects always "come back to their own places silent and unsmiling." In Spicer's letter to Lorca, emotion must itself become an "encysted" object, only then to be transferred to the poem.

Spicer's distrust of personal expression is one of the strongest contributing factors to his privileging of the "book" or serial poem over individual lyrics. In his letter to Robin Blaser in *Admonitions*, he declares that most of his poetry prior to *After Lorca* looks "foul": "The poems belong nowhere. They are one night stands filled (the best of them) with their own emotion, but pointing nowhere, as meaningless as sex in a Turkish bath." As a compositional procedure, seriality is meant to free the individual poem from its status of "one night stand"; the resonance of poem against poem in the series creates what Blaser, in his essay "The Fire," calls "a narrative which refuses to adopt an imposed story line, and completes itself only in the sequence of poems...a sequence of energies which runs out when so much of the tale is told." From poem to poem, the series moves forward through its own urgencies; there is less opportunity for the individual's feelings, as Spicer says, "to be converted into poetry as one would exchange foreign money." Spicer's book as haunted house creates, according to Peter Riley, "a narrative out of the discrete singularities of the person, when those singularities represented the only field in which the person could operate as himself."

Finding the means by which "the person could operate as himself" and yet remain free of the ego's affective constraints is a task which preoccupies the poets of the San Francisco Renaissance and their colleagues across the country at Black Mountain. Olson's solution is total dedication to verbal kinetics and process, as is clear in *Projective Verse*: "get on with it, keep moving, keep in, speed, the nerves, their speed, the perceptions, theirs, the acts, the split second acts, the whole business, keep it moving as fast as you can, citizen." Spicer's alternative is that of dictation, "being filled up by whatever's outside," the occasions when "things happen simply because the poem wants them to happen." Dictation, which Spicer decisively links to serial composition, is usually discussed in the Vancouver Lectures as a sort of negative theology: it's not Creeley following the dictation of language; not Duncan on words and their shadows; not Olson, plugging into linguistic energy; not Williams' magic of objects. In fact, Spicer's notion of dictation is profoundly Romantic, as is indicated by his use of the last Romantic, W. B. Yeats, as his model for a poet who took dictation from the outside, the first to do so since Blake. It seems that Spicer needs to draw on a Romantic notion of inspiration in order to resist what he perceives to be an equally Romantic notion of self-expression.

Spicer's suspicion of authorial agency and his concomitant faith in dictation, all so representative of his generation's struggle to accept the task of the traditional lyricist, leads to deeply ironic results, for Spicer's poetry grows all the more personal the more programmatic its dictated seriality becomes. Beneath its abrasive tonal surface, the plaintive ghost of melancholy, 'even despairing lyricism may still be heard, and it is just this sense of pained loss which resonates from poem to poem. As he says toward the end of his last work, the *Book of Magazine Verse*,

The poem begins to mirror itself.
The identity of the poet gets more obvious.
Why can't we sing songs like nightingales? Because we're not
     nightingales and can never become them. The poet has an
     arid parch of his reality and the others.
Things desert him. I thought of you as a butterfly tonight with
     clipped wings. (265)

It takes Spicer till the end of his career to realize that we can't sing songs like nightingales, that a spontaneous relation to the "outside" is impossible for the human subject, laden with the consciousness of failure and the knowledge of mortality. Like Keats before him, Spicer finally acknowledges that an unmediated relation of the singer to the song cannot be. In Keats, the outside is nature, and the immortal song of the nightingale is heard by one burdened human generation after the next. In Spicer, the outside is an occulted vision of what he calls in *After Lorca* "the real," which by the time he writes the *Book of Magazine Verse* is no longer full of juicy lemons and beautiful young men, but rather has "an arid parch" to it. The utopian desire for a "thing language," in which objects give of themselves to words freely and immediately (as in the lovely poem "Duet for a Chair and a Table") likewise fails, as "Things desert him." In short, neither a Romantic nor an Objectivist relation to the external world can sustain the poet when what he has to say comes from the heart. As he declares in the poem just prior to the one I have cited, "If this is dictation, it is driving/Me wild."

In comparison with Spicer, his friend and sparring partner Robert Duncan is never driven wild by dictation: there is, at least in my hearing, a sort of disinterestedness or impersonality to even Duncan's most ecstatic moments which differs significantly from Spicer's pained struggles. Duncan is a genuinely prophetic poet, a voice of *kosmos*; his magian aspirations scandalized Spicer, for whom dictation, or inspiration, is always a matter of demonic possession rather than the theurgic invocation it is in Duncan.

In *Unending Design*, Joseph Conte notes that Spicer begins thinking about the serial poem in relation to Duncan's *Medieval Scenes*. In Spicer's letter to Robin Blaser in *Admonitions*, he says that Duncan taught "not to search for the perfect poem but to let your way of writing of the moment go along its own paths, explore and retreat but never be fully realized (confined) within the boundaries of one poem." Conte then draws the important distinction between the finite serial form of Spicer's books, and the infinite serial form of Duncan's *Passages*—though I should note that early Duncan works, like *Medieval Scenes*, and even later ones like "Apprehensions" are finite series as Conte would define the form. For Spicer, the finite structure of the book or the series that definitely ends produces internal "resonances," for poems should "echo and reecho against each other." On the other hand, Duncan's infinite or totally open work is based on his notion that "I enter the poem as I entered my own life, moving between an initiation and a terminus I cannot name." And indeed, this lifelong apprehension of initiation without determinate closure is to be felt even in Duncan's works with identifiable endings; in this respect, all of his poems, as he says in the introduction to *Bending the Bow*, "belong to a series that extends in an area larger than my work in them." Consider these lines from "A Set of Romantic Hymns" in *Roots and Branches*:

> Fountain of forms!   Life springs of unique being!
>
> Never again this sequence I am.
> Never again this one hand.
>   drawing its song from men's words.
>
> Never again this one life, this
>   universe bent to this lyre
>   he would make in the language
>   for music's sake.
>
> Never again just this derivation
>   from manhood, these numbers,
>   this dwelling in the shape of things.

Appearing in a set of Romantic hymns, these verses extend the lyric tradition toward which they self-consciously gesture. Duncan's poetry tends to coalesce around discrete lyric nodes, rapturous moments which flash out in his increasingly diffuse verbal *kosmos*. If in Spicer's work, the utterance strains to depart from self-expression, only to be tugged back into heartfelt lament, then in Duncan's poetry, the utterance expresses itself by flying beyond itself; it is, as he declares, "Never again this one life," "Never again just this derivation." In Spicer, the destabilization of lyricism through dictated messages is a retrograde motion. In Duncan, lyricism is destabilized by projection to its furthest extreme; in its flight or passage, it is never itself, never a single derivation but a continuous process of derivation. In Spicer, the lyric self longs for decreation, but ironically it is recreated through every experience of verbal interruption and discontinuity. In Duncan, the lyric self is found through polysemous dispersion; the more "this one life" is lost in strains of universal music, the more that music is made ineluctably its own.

Thus the horizontal trajectory of the serial poem, subject to frequent rupture in Spicer's case, and to continuous weaving and unweaving in Duncan's, remains in productive tension with the vertically oriented, momentary singularity of the traditional lyric. Following these developments, more recent poets accept the challenge in the unresolved, productive tension between serial form and lyric utterance. The serial work of Michael Palmer, for instance, however different in tone from Jack Spicer's, continues to be haunted by the palpable absence of the lyric occasion and the concomitant presence of disruptive, seemingly dictated, and frighteningly uncanny voices. *Baudelaire Series*, in the volume *Sun*, is one of the clearest examples of this condition in Palmer, and it is also—not accidentally, I believe—one of his greatest achievements to date.

Baudelaire, according to Walter Benjamin, is the first poet fully to face the problem of lyricism under the conditions of modernity; thus he is naturally the tutelary spirit or *daemon* of Palmer's work. According to Benjamin, "Baudelaire patterned his image of the artist after an image of the hero," because "it takes a heroic constitution to live modernism." Yet as Benjamin demonstrates repeatedly, the posture of the heroic lyricist is continually undermined by modernity; or as Spicer will say years later, "Heros eat soup like anyone else." The decay of the lyric aura since *Les Fleurs du Mal* is, in effect, Palmer's unvoiced theme in *Baudelaire Series*; hence the ghostly appearances in the text of other major lyric figures of the century, including Rilke, Celan, Vallejo, Creeley and Duncan. This essay does not permit a full examination of the series in the context of progressive auratic loss, so I will limit myself to a look at the proem:

> *A hundred years ago I made a book*
> *and in that book I left a spot*
> *and on that spot I placed a seme*
>
> *with the mechanism of the larynx*
> *around an inky center*
> *leading forward-backward*
>
> *into snow-sun*
> *then to frozen sun itself*
> *Threads and nerves have brought us to a house*

and clouds called crescent birds are a lifting song
No need to sail further
protesting here and there against some measures

across the years of codes and names
always immortal as long as you remain a man
eating the parts of him indicated by the prophets

stomach skull and gullet
bringing back the lost state
Yes I dreamed another dream and nobody was in it

Baudelaire's (and Palmer's) book contains a spot, a place that is also a seme or sign, which in turn corresponds to "the mechanism of the larynx," the voice or phonocentric utterance of the subject enunciating itself. But this spot/seme/voice is to be found around an "inky" or written center which is really no center at all: writing decenters the self, contradictorily "leading backward-forward//into sun-snow." Baudelaire's notorious spleen ("nerves"), the condition of lyricism frustrated by a hostile modern environment, in addition to his theory of correspondences ("threads" or relations between words and things) lead to "a lifting song" of Romantic transcendence. Yet for Palmer, like Baudelaire himself, the worth of such transcendence is questionable: "the years of codes and names" which constitute the history of poetry promise immortality for the individual poet, but only at the price of heroic self-sacrifice, the martyrdom of self-expression and the ritual cannibalization or consumption by generations of readers who "immortalize" the life and canonize the poems. This, it would appear, is the only means through which the poet intent upon "bringing back the lost state," the lyric harmony of self, word and world, can achieve anything near his goal. But as the poem ends, another possibility opens: "Yes I just dreamed another dream and nobody was in it." Suddenly the heroic stance of Romanticism and modernism gives way to postmodernism: the dream of the text continues but it is a dream of absence; no self at all is to be found.

It is just this condition—dreaming or semiotic activity somehow devoid of the dreamer or poet—which Palmer explores in the rest of his series. Some lines from the next few poems:

> Words say, Misspell and misspell your name
> Words say, Leave this life
>
> . . .
>
> Dear Lexicon, I died in you . . .
> Dear Lexia, There is no mind
> Dear Book, You were never a book
>
> . . .
>
> If we're really mirrors in a poem
> what will we call this song

Linguistic self-expression is regarded as an impossibility in these poems. Words lead us out of ourselves, into a deathlike state of loss. Words lead us elsewhere; like Rilke's torso of an archaic Apollo, words order us to leave our lives behind, to change our lives—though unlike the statue, words are inherently unstable and continually unmake themselves. But paradoxically, it is out of this unmaking, this sequence of decreative gestures, that the lyric tradition is recalled. Inthe first stanza of the last poem, we hear that "Nowness and nowness sings the crow/Whatness and whiteness sings the center/Then and then signs the hen." The natural world signifies the here and now, but reminds us of the past as well. The center, once inky, is now a whiteness. Inky or white, its singing remains, however decentered its singer has become.

Seriality, then, implies the simultaneous dissolution and recovery of the self as singer in the continuum of the song. Traditional lyric subjectivity may have come to an impasse, but the serial poem, conceived through a process of dictation, has proven an appropriate corrective. Rather than expose the "big lie" of the personal, the serial poem provides us with something of much greater value: a structure and an aesthetic through which the self and its concomitant lyric utterance can be redefined and resituated in a new and variously decentered discursive landscape.

In this context, the last poet I would like to discuss is Nathaniel Mackey. If in Palmer's *Baudelaire Series*, seriality provides the necessary structure for an endlessly rehearsed, Spicerian evacuation of lyric material, then in Mackey's *School of Udhra*, Duncan's continual weaving and unweaving of serial poetry is taken to its furthest extreme. Like Duncan's later work, *School of Udhra* consists of various open series begun in Mackey's previous volume, *Eroding Witness*. One series in particular, *"mu"*, nomadically wanders through various sections of the work like Duncan's *Passages*, producing, in Duncan's words quoted by Mackey as an epigraph, "a continent of feeling beyond our feeling." But to an even greater extent than Duncan, the verbal texture of Mackey's writing is so much of a piece, despite (or because of) its almost total fragmentation and lack of finished sentences, that the effect is of a single utterance broken almost arbitrarily into individual poems.

In these poems, personal experience is always falling back and blending into myth, *muthos*, which, as Jane Harrison in Mackey's other epigraph observes, possibly "was simply the introjectional utterance *mu*." And Mackey's *"mu"* is certainly filled with introjectional utterances, which one associates with either sexual contact or divine revelation. The fulfillment of desire or the discovery of divinity in the other are both experiences which dissolve the sense of self, producing what Mackey calls the "non-pronominal ought," a self-consciously utopian state or "New utopic/thought no sooner/there than discarded." Mackey's poetry, like Duncan's, consists of a discarding of language in the perpetual hope of and movement toward linguistic presence, only to be glimpsed, never to be achieved. The passages of sexual union and of mythic divinity produce the simultaneous revelation and disappearance of the "City of spirit we/lost our way toward. Utopia/ lost in the mind."

In an insightful essay which appears in the Mackey issue of *Talisman*, Joseph Donahue notes that in Mackey's poetry, "the elided first person singular takes on an unexpected thematic significance. The utopian ambition of the poem requires the poet to evade constantly the pronominal hell of the sentence, since . . .that is the site where actor and acted upon are locked into place. Yet the urgency with which he must configure fatedness thrusts the poet always toward uttering sentences. A "hidden I," nowhere named, is everywhere implied as the

poet conjures sentences he is reluctant to complete." Donahue's observation of a 'hidden I' which is related to the poem's "utopian ambition"
confirms my own sense that the pronominal dispersion in Mackey's
work functions under contemporary cultural conditions in a way that
is analogous to the expressive subject of more traditional lyric poetry.
Donahue states that "As readers we are potential members of what the
poet calls a 'sprung polity', cut loose from a narrowly construed identity in a world where to name actors is to create a social order where
one is acted upon, where an 'I' becomes a 'he', a 'we' becomes a 'they.'"
Because for many poets today, the assertion of lyric subjectivity in its
quest for transcendence is no longer a tenable vehicle for poetry's
utopian impulse (as it was in much Romantic poetry), the lyric subject
"disappears." Nevertheless, its absence or invisibility may be as effec-
tive as its presence, as in these quotes from two different parts of *"mu"*:

His they their
we, their he
his was but if
need be one,

          self-
extinguishing
I, neither sham nor
excuse yet an
alibi, exited,

          out,

                else

the only where
he'd be.

   . . .

      . . . Arced encounter,

                covered
we were and by that
touched "I-ness" to "I-ness,"
      inward, wombed inducement

arced into "us-ness,"
otherness, nothingness . . .

For Mackey—and I believe, many other poets today—the "I" is neither sham nor excuse, yet must be "self-extinguished," must exit, so that a plurality of pronominal utterances may be heard as one. Writing in this dictated fashion is, in a sense, like making love, as "I-ness" touches "I-ness" to produce an other, an "arced encounter" which passes into a blissful nothingness that is all.

"LYRICAL INTERFERENCE"
IN *THE NEW AMERICAN POETRY*

In "*The New American Poetry* Revisited, Again," Alan Golding carefully analyzes the construction of Donald Allen's famous anthology, delving into the archives to demonstrate that "*The New American Poetry*'s ongoing interest for literary historians is precisely that it provides a conflicted rather than homogeneous picture, not of 'the' postwar avant-garde but of multiple avant-garde communities." My concern here, as in the case of the other essays in this volume, is less literary history than poetics, both theoretical and practical, but any discussion of "the poetics of *The New American Poetry*" (which actually became the title for Allen's followup collection) cannot help but draw upon Golding's definitive article. "As regards writing practice," Golding states, "*The New American Poetry*, more than any other anthology, helped promote and canonize ideas of field composition based on Charles Olson's 'Projective Verse'; a (re)definition of poetic form as immanent and processual; a poetics of dailiness and of the personal (as distinct from the confessional); and a poetry of humor and play (as distinct from wit). It is *the* anthology, in short, that marked the early postmodern turn, in Charles Altieri's terms, 'from symbolist thought to immanence.' And it retains enough staying power as an anthological touchstone for alternative poetries that editors of avant-garde anthologies continue to invoke it as a model over thirty years after its publication."

What does Golding's historical interpretation imply for those poets of the present generation who still look back to *The New American Poetry*, not merely as an "anthological touchstone" but as a matrix, however conflicted its origins, of a writing practice from which we may still learn today? Over forty years have passed since the Allen anthology went head to head with its "academic" antithesis, the Hall, Pack, and Simpson *New Poets of England and America*, a contest which has since been recapitulated in seemingly endless anthology wars featuring language poetry (supposedly the inheritor of the New Americans' avant-garde mantle), new formalism, and the capacious, ill-defined poetic "mainstream" that feeds *The New Yorker* and *American Poetry Review*. These conflicts have had their commentators in their turn. I wish to step back from this history as much as possible, however (knowing full well that I have gone a few rounds in these critical dustups), in order to recapture, albeit with greater self-consciousness, a sense of the power, authority, and magic that I felt in the early seventies, when, as an undergraduate, I was writing poetry furiously and, as I mentioned elsewhere in this volume, schlepping around *The New American Poetry* as if it were Holy Writ. In doing so, I want to consider a crucial poetic notion that the Allen anthology calls into question: the idea that poetic lyricism serves as an apt—indeed, one of the greatest—artistic vehicles for subjective expression.

In his preface to *The New American Poetry*, Allen states simply that the poetry published in his anthology "has shown one common characteristic: a total rejection of all those qualities typical of academic verse. Following the practice and precepts of Ezra Pound and William Carlos Williams, it has built on their achievements and gone on to evolve new conceptions of the poem." The poet who most obviously attempts to synthesize the practice and precepts of those precursors is, of course, Charles Olson; and in giving pride of place to Olson in *The New American Poetry*, both as practitioner and theorist, Allen in effect presents him as the single most influential experimental poet of the postwar period. To be sure, Olson rejects "all those qualities typical of academic verse." More specifically, in his insistence on an open poetry based on such notions as process and field composition, as codified in "Projective Verse," Olson has a direct or indirect effect on virtually all the other poets in Allen's anthology, an effect that in most instances predates the construction of the anthology itself. In arguing for Olson's influence and representative status, I must downplay Allen's original categorization of Black Mountain School, San Francisco Renaissance, Beat Generation and New York School: though many important distinctions can be drawn among these various groupings, I am concerned with a more fundamental difference and an older, more traditional poetic issue—the status of the lyric—which is reformulated in Olson's work and which is felt throughout what is now broadly known as "the new American poetry."

In "Projective Verse," Olson defines "objectism" (his version of the objectivism with which Pound and Williams were variously involved) as "the getting rid of the lyrical interference of the individual as ego, of the 'subject' and his soul." For Olson, "a man is himself an object," and "if he stays inside himself, if he is contained within his nature as he is participant in the larger force, he will be able to listen, and his hearing through himself will give him secrets objects share." In some respects, this is a reworking through objectivism of Keats' negative capability, "when man is capable of being in uncertainties, Mysteries, doubts, without any irritable reaching after fact & reason." Keats is one of Olson's heroes; he is invoked at the beginning of "Projective Verse" in his opposition to Milton's and Wordsworth's "egotistical sublime." As one of the first poets to articulate the loss of the ego through composition as indeterminate, experiential process, Keats, at least according to Olson, anticipates the projective notion of the poet as object in a field of objects, open to the flux of being. Subjective expression of the individual soul or ego, which Olson associates with lyricism, must be replaced by a poetry of greater scope and objectivity. The poet who adheres to lyric subjectivity "shall find little to sing but himself," but "if projective verse is practiced long enough, is driven ahead hard enough along the course I think it dictates, verse again can carry much larger material than it has carried in our language since the Elizabethans."

When we consider Olson's own poetry, we see that he is almost always more involved with narrative, exhortation, and the historical and mythical dimensions of epic than with the lyric mode. Looking only at Allen's selection of Olson's verse (which, according to Tom Clark in his biography, Olson regarded as rather tame), we see that even the most personal utterances, "Maximus, to himself" and "As the Dead Prey Upon Us," are not particularly lyrical; rather, they represent Olson's discursive struggle to get outside of himself and achieve some manner of integration with social being:

The nets of being
are only eternal if you sleep as your hands
ought to be busy. Method, method
I too call on you to come
to the aid of all men, to women most
who know most, to woman to tell
men to awake. Awake men,
awake

The muscular syntax and strained enjambment in this typical passage from "As the Dead Prey Upon Us" are more indicative of public
argument than intimate song. In short, even when focused on his own
predicaments, Olson is always addressing the polis.

But this is not the case for many of the other poets in Allen's
anthology. Among Olson's colleagues and disciples, as well as other figures who read Olson sympathetically but were not in personal contact,
are a wide range of poets with a serious investment in the expressiveness of "the 'subject' and his soul." As Frank O'Hara cries at the end
of his magnificent "Hotel Transylvanie," punctuating his line with
Olson's signature slash mark, but I hold on/I am lyrical to a fault/I do
not despair being too foolish where will you find me, projective verse,
since I will be gone?

O'Hara is camping it up here, as is his wont, but these lines
nonetheless raise the question with which I am most concerned: what
happens to the lyric impulse when forced to confront a position so
strongly opposed to subjective expression and personalized rhapsody?
"You just go on your nerve" says O'Hara in his sly "Personism" mani-
festo, but even for the poet who turned nonchalance into an art, this
advice is not enough. Personism, according to O'Hara, "does not have
to do with personality or intimacy . . . It puts the poem squarely
between the poet and the person [that is, the person addressed in the
poem], Lucky Pierre style, and the poem is correspondingly gratified."
Note that it is the poem, the art object, that is "gratified": as in Olson's

case, the composition (in the double sense of process and product) counts for more than personal expression, "sustaining the poet's feelings towards the poem while preventing love from distracting him into feeling about the person." As personal and intimate as much of O'Hara's poetry appears, it is not, in the conventional sense, self-expression. Its lyricism, if we may apply the term to this work, is derived from the form of O'Hara's experience rather than his feelings, which are as much a source of "lyrical interference" for him as they are for Olson. As he says in his statement in *The New American Poetry*, "What is happening to me, allowing for lies and exaggerations which I try to avoid, goes into my poems. I don't think my experiences are clarified or made beautiful for myself or anyone else, they are just there in whatever form I can find them."

Poems, then, are forms of experience found through experience, an insight that O'Hara practically allegorizes in "Why I Am Not a Painter," with its refrain "days go by" and its gradual discovery of the forms of Mike Goldberg's painting and of O'Hara's own poem:

> . . . One day I am thinking of
> a color: orange. I write a line
> about orange. Pretty soon it is a
> whole page of words, not lines.
> Then another page. There should be
> so much more, not of orange, of
> words, of how terrible orange is
> and life. Days go by. . . .

Can lived experience be a making, a *poesis*? Can our feelings in the midst of life be experienced so as to be that which is not only lived, but made? These questions seem to be asked by all the poets in *The New American Poetry*, regardless of the emotional register in which they write. Perhaps what Olson is so concerned about when he criticizes the poet's fixation on soul is actually a falsely transcendental lyricism, a staging of lofty feelings rather than the discovery of real feelings through the search for form. "That the poet cannot afford to traffick in any other 'sign' than his own, his self, the man or woman he is," Olson warns Duncan in "Against Wisdom As Such." "Otherwise God does rush in." Or as O'Hara says in "Personism" about the technical aspect of writing, "There's nothing metaphysical about it. Unless, of course, you flatter yourself into thinking that what you're experiencing is 'yearning.'"

Yearning, whether for a beloved other or some transcendental condition, is one of the more private emotions an individual can feel; but ironically, it is also one of those emotions most frequently expressed in lyric poetry. It could even be said that lyric poetry is predicated on this irony, as language at its most intense is put in the service of what is understood to be ineffable feeling. If lyrical interference is a sort of self-flattery, as O'Hara implies, then Olson & Co. are certainly right to inveigh against it. Nevertheless, a yearning lyricism pervades much of the work in *The New American Poetry*, against which Olson's theories and personal influence may serve as a necessary counter-pressure, a Yeatsian mask or anti-self. Two of Olson's closest associates, Robert Creeley and Robert Duncan, are essentially lyric poets who work hard, in both their essays and poems, to accommodate themselves to an anti-expressive aesthetic. In Duncan's formulations, rhapsodic expressions of transcendental yearning become magical language-events that reach beyond the individual, the ego, the soul. As he declares in *The Truth & Life of Myth*, "Speaking of a thing I call upon its name, and the Name takes over from me the story I would tell, if I let the dimmest realization of that power enter here. But the myth we are telling is the myth of the Power of the Word. The Word, as we refer to It, undoes all the bounds of semantics we would draw in Its creative need to realize Its true Self. It takes over." Creeley, on the other hand, produces an intensely personal (but not, as Golding distinguishes, confessional) poetry that is charged with such "humilitas" that even the most intimate, lyrical gestures are rendered in objective terms. Thus, as he puts it in "A Note," "I look to words, and nothing else, for my own redemption either as man or poet. . . . I mean then *words*—as opposed to content. I care what the poem says, only as a poem—I am no longer interested in the exterior attitude toward which the poem may well point, as signboard." In each instance, language is posed against the expression of individual feeling.

But rather than pursue this line of argument in regard to Creeley and Duncan, whose work has received so much attention over the years, I will briefly consider two other, less discussed poets in the Allen anthology, John Wieners and Helen Adam. Among the Black Mountain poets, Wieners was one of Olson's most devoted student-disciples, while Adam, grouped with the San Francisco Renaissance poets, seems so remote from the experimentalism of *The New American Poetry* that at first glance, one might wonder why her work was anthologized there at all.

In his essay on Wieners' *Selected Poems*, Creeley notes that Olson spoke of his student's work as "'a poetry of affect', by which I took him to mean a poetry that is the process of a life being lived . . . In other words, the art becomes the complex process of a 'making real' all that one is given to live." This in itself is fairly typical of the way poets in the Allen anthology view the relationship of poetic composition to life. But even among the wild and often self-destructive lives in that quintessential fifties gathering, Wieners was an extremist: mental illness, drug addiction, a particularly tortured homosexuality turned him into a legend, a scandalous rumor, and as Allen Ginsberg says, "a man reduced to loneness in poetry, without worldly distraction—and a man become one with his poetry." *The Hotel Wentley Poems*, named for the residential hotel in San Francisco, appeared in 1958, when Wieners was twenty-four. Poets took notice: "everybody here is running around after dull pleasantries and/wondering if *The Hotel Wentley Poems* is as great as I say it is." So writes Frank O'Hara in his poem "Les Luths," dated October 6, 1959. Shortly thereafter, Allen republished five of the eight poems in that short first book as Wieners' section in *The New American Poetry*.

At its uncanny best, Wieners' poetry simultaneously achieves intimacy and distance, a condition Creeley struggles to describe in discussing this work. "How is it far if you think it?" asks Creeley, citing "a purported Chinese apothegm." In the terms I'm using here, Wieners shows both a total commitment to and a total disregard for "the 'subject' and his soul": the I is another, but its expressiveness is not to be denied. Wieners' is not an anti-lyricism, as one finds so often in Jack

Spicer; nor does it employ the klutzy yet graceful sleight-of-hand irony that distinguishes so many of Creeley's lyrics. Yet Creeley's admiration for the final section of "A Poem for Painters" aligns the two poets:

> At last. I come to the last defense.
>
> > My poems contain no
> > wilde beestes, no
> > lady of the lake, music
> > of the spheres, or organ chants.
> >
> > Only the score of a man's
> > struggle to stay with
> > what is his own, what
> > lies within him to do.
> >
> > Without which is nothing.
> > And I come to this
> > knowing the waste,
> >
> > leaving the rest up to love
> > and its twisted faces,
> > my hands claw out at
> > only to draw back from the
> > blood already running there.

The lyric tradition is, in effect, held under erasure here; the "lady of the lake" (and Wieners' poetry, like Creeley's and Duncan's, is actually full of such ladies) is affirmed through denial; and love's bloody power over the subject, its intimacy and wrenching otherness, is confronted directly in the poem's last lines. That some of the most crucial lines ("Only the score of a man's/struggle to stay with/what is his own, what/lies within him, to do") are pure Olson both in their argument and syntax indicates the degree to which Wieners is able to assimilate the aesthetic of "Projective Verse" to the renewed subjectivity of his project. Wieners' finest work still lay ahead of him in his two subsequent volumes, *Ace of Pentacles* (1964) and *Nerves* (1970). But *The Hotel Wentley Poems* already demonstrates the ways in which poets allied with Olson were reconsidering the status of the lyric.

At the farthest extreme from Olson's position in *The New American Poetry* is the inimitable Scottish poet Helen Adam. A child prodigy who published her first book of ballads at age twelve to national acclaim, Adam was thirty when she immigrated to the United States in 1939 with her mother and sister. Settling in San Francisco in 1953, she became a central figure in the San Francisco Renaissance. For Robert Duncan, Adam, both as writer and performer, "opened the door to the full heritage of the forbidden romantics." I have discussed Adam's version of romanticism in *The Utopian Moment*; here I only wish to ask whether her traditional poetic in any way relates to the conflicted lyricism in *The New American Poetry*. In other words, is it only her participation in the San Francisco literary milieu that links her work to the experimental poetry in the Allen anthology? My answer, briefly, is no: in one important respect, Adam's verse represents as little investment in the ego as can be found in any of the poetry in the anthology. What Duncan says of her poems makes this clear: "They were entirely concerned with event, with marvelous event; nowhere was the language shaded to hint at the poet's sensibility." Thus we may distinguish lyric utterance from the shadings of personal sensibility. If there is anything of Adam's "soul" in her ballads (and of course there must be), it is wholly dissolved in the passion of her narratives and the hypnotic music of her rhymes:

> The hair rushed in. He struggled and tore, but whenever he tore a
> > tress,
> "I love my love with a capital Z," sang the hair of the sorceress.
> It swarmed about him, it swaddled him fast, it muffled his every
> > groan.
> Like a golden monster it seized his flesh, and then it sought the
> > bone,
> Ha! Ha!
> And then it sought the bone.

Olson could not have had Adam's "I Love My Love" in mind when he wrote "Projective Verse," but he was thinking of the qualities that give the ballad form its power. After quoting "Western Wynd," one of the oldest English ballads, he challenges his readers and warns them that "to step back here to this place of the elements and minims of language, is to engage speech where it is least careless—and least logical." Little did he know that at least one of his contemporaries was already there, producing a poetry of verbal precision and unbridled, magical passion. Allen only included "I Love My Love" in *The New American Poetry*, thinking, as Golding notes, that a little of her work went a long way. This may be why Duncan devoted an entire paragraph to her power over him in his biographical note, confessing that "in admitting her genius, I was able to shake off at last the modern proprieties—originality, style, currency of language, sensibility and integrity. I have a great appetite for approval from whatever source, and only the example of this poet who cares nothing for opinions but all for the life of the imagination, for the marvellous that is the grain of living poetry, saves me at times." In effect, what Olson finds in "Western Wynd" Duncan finds in Helen Adam, a quality which in each instance opens the poet to the imaginative resources of language that carry the poem far beyond his or her individual concerns.

In a certain respect, the poetry of Adam and Wieners—still under-read, still undervalued—symbolizes the achievement of *The New American Poetry* to an even greater extent than the fully sustained careers of more famous figures from the anthology, such as Creeley, Duncan, Levertov, Ginsberg, Ashbery, and Snyder—and, of course, Olson himself. (The enduring influence of O'Hara and Spicer, despite their deaths in mid-career, is a miracle of a different order.) For me, that achievement lies in the radical refunctioning of the lyric impulse under what we now call the conditions of postmodernity, a refunctioning in which much was gained, and much lost. "Our age bereft of nobility," begins Wieners' "Poem for Painters," stating the problem succinctly; "Only/in the poem/comes an image—that we rule/the line by the pen." Seeking a new contract between lyric interiority and the instantaneous sensation of the exterior world ("ONE PERCEPTION MUST IMMEDIATELY AND DIRECTLY LEAD TO A FURTHER PER-CEPTION" demands Olson of the composing poet), an entire genera-tion of practitioners pushed their art (and often enough, their lives) to the limit, and the result was an astonishing bounty of poetry. Critics have often observed that one dimension of this poetry's "postmod-ernism" consists of the reintegration of a romantic sensibility with a modernist understanding of form, a synthesis that is explicit in the work of Duncan, but is actually apparent to a greater or lesser extent in nearly every poet who appears in the anthology. (This notion informs my analyses of the New York School and the San Francisco Renaissance in *The Utopian Moment*.) This *zeitgeist* was felt by major and minor talents alike, and in more than one instance, it elevated voices starting out in the most unpromising circumstances to signifi-cant utterance. "I am showered by the scent/of the finished line," con-tinues Wieners in his grand poem of election: out of ordinary circum-stances, at once harrowing and mundane, comes a verbal authority that beautifully coordinates erotic love and poetic desire, bringing them together in an open form that is still, however paradoxically, "fin-ished." Poem after poem in *The New American Poetry* attains to this state, as if Donald Allen had searched specifically for those examples in the work of each poet in which lyricism proves to be not "interference" but an exalted version of the process through which we perceive imme-diate experience: "practically a blaze of pure sensibility," as O'Hara puts it in the appropriately titled "In Favor of One's Time."

In "Projective Verse," Olson links his critique of "lyrical interfer-ence" with what he believes to be an exhausted or outmoded concep-tion of individual subjectivity, and the "objectism" he endorses instead is linked in turn with the "projective" or processual act of writing itself. At full throttle, poets like Olson, O'Hara or Ginsberg reach toward the sublime. The sheer rush of their language, reflecting their total engage-ment with the objective conditions of reality, produces what Olson calls "the *kinetics* of the thing": "a high energy-construct and, at all points, an energy-discharge." The risk of this procedure, and the problem to which nearly all these poets are susceptible, is, simply, *incoherence*. It could well be that Olson suspects as much: in his privileging "the speech-force of language" in the poem, he acknowledges that the poem's various elements will be allowed "their proper confusions." But poetry is not confusion, although it may be derived from unintelligible experiences or states of mind, and that is why, incidentally, Olson was mistaken to place such a great emphasis on speech, breath, and so on— if poetry were primarily speech, then everyone would be a poet. Zukofsky (who thought Olson had stolen from his writings on objectivism) is closer to the truth when he notes in "A" that his poetic is "An integral/Lower limit speech/Upper limit music." Between those limits the poet seeks a form. The incoherence of the inner life and the incoherence of external reality can be reconciled, but in the increasing complexity of postmodernity, the task grows ever more difficult. Olson himself understood this; as he declares with great pathos in "As the Dead Prey Upon Us,"

> The desperateness is, that the instant
> which is also paradise (paradise
> is happiness) dissolves
> into the next instant, and power
> flows to meet the next occurrence

Let these lines stand for both the struggle and the achievement of *The New American Poetry*.

BRONK, DUNCAN,
AND THE FAR BORDER OF POETRY

Literary historians and critics concerned with matters of poetic influence are bound to have a difficult time with William Bronk. The foremost of his modern precursors are Frost and Stevens. His mentor at Dartmouth (he graduated in 1938) was Frost's friend Sidney Cox; from Frost's poetry and Cox's teaching he soon developed what Ruth Grogan calls "a colloquiality which uncannily undermines its own apparent hominess." Stevens was a somewhat later influence, but by 1946 Bronk was reading him carefully, and many of the poems in *Light and Dark* (1956) and *The World, the Worldless* (1964), the books in which Bronk moves rapidly toward maturity, are marked by Stevens's characteristically abstract language.

Bronk's other early literary associations, however, are somewhat different. Correspondence with Robert Creeley led to contact with Cid Corman and Bronk's eventual publication in *Origin,* a seminal journal of the Black Mountain group and of the "New American Poetry." He shared a strong interest in Pre-Columbian civilizations with another important contributor to *Origin,* Charles Olson, though their treatment of the Pre-Columbian theme, and of course, their basic styles, differ dramatically. Bronk's publication in *Origin* brought him to the attention of George Oppen; correspondence and friendship led to the publication of *The World, the Worldless*, put out jointly by New Directions and June Oppen Degnan's *San Francisco Review.*

This brief summary of Bronk's early literary biography raises an interesting problem. Admired by such figures as Creeley, Olson, Oppen and Corman, Bronk's work, emerging from that of Frost and Stevens, presumably has little to do with the Objectivists or the Black Mountain group, which trace their origins back to two very different modern poets — Pound and Williams. "There are no ideas in things... Take this,

William Carlos," jokes Bronk in conversation, after a reading "The Annihilation of Matter." About Pound—pointedly—he has nothing to say. Why then did followers of Pound and Williams seek Bronk out, publish him, and espouse his poetry? Some skeptics might argue that this entanglement of interests and ancestors only demonstrates how fruitless the study of affinities and influences will prove in attempting to understand the achievement of any one particular poet. But affinities and influences reveal concerns which go beyond the particular figures, beyond the biographies and histories, even beyond the dialectics of influence as studied by such critics as Harold Bloom.

In order to demonstrate what I mean, I propose to set Bronk's work against that of another poet who is much closer to the traditions of Pound and Williams, to the Black Mountain group and to the Objectivists: Robert Duncan. I would like to compare Bronk's methods and ideas to those of Duncan, a comparison which, I believe, will describe part of the far border of poetry in our time. We will find that in some respects their projects run parallel to each other, heading in the same direction—that far border of poetry—yet without the technical and conceptual wherewithal for discovering common ground. But I also think that each writer's project contains within itself some of the same concerns as the other, though addressed in very different epistemological and discursive modes.

These concerns arise from what both poets implicitly understand as "the crisis in American verse." The phrase is Stephen Fredman's, and as he explains, "The root meaning of 'crisis'—discrimination or decision, a necessary decision—describes the situation of American poetry, which, in a strict sense, has always been in crisis, always called upon to make necessary existential decisions. . . . The decision to write an American poetry is always crucial, always existential, never merely a case of deciding upon a subject matter and a verse form. When the primary issue in writing poetry shifts from the choice of matter and meter to the decision as to whether poetry, under present conditions, is possible, then that poetry can truly be spoken of as in crisis." In *Poet's Prose*, Fredman's understanding of this crisis leads to an extraordinary exploration of the problem of genre, a problem which for him is mediated by American poets' frequent recourse to prose. This turn to prose is indicative not only of the American desire for freedom, but the specific freedom to "make a statement—to interrogate the realm of truth" in a way that the aesthetic tradition of the European lyric could not. The problem of poetic genre—an American problem, a modern problem—is thus an epistemological problem, a methodological problem and an existential problem. In other words: What can the poem know? What can the poem do? What can the poem be?

These questions are answered in one way (if such questions are ever "answered") when an American poet turns to prose. But the cases of Duncan and Bronk, although both of them surely seek to interrogate the realm of truth, and both of them do write "poet's prose" at crucial moments in their careers, are different. Simply put, Bronk and Duncan are poets who remain wedded to the lyric tradition and, concomitantly, to the experience and articulation of the sublime. I follow Thomas Weiskel in his book on the Romantic sublime in my understanding of the sublime as the experience of transcending the human "in feeling and in speech," and of the Romantic sublime, so important to Bronk and Duncan, as "a massive transposition of transcendence into a naturalistic key; in short, a stunning metaphor."

Yet Bronk and Duncan both understand, as does John Ashbery, a poet with somewhat more tenuous links to the lyric sublime, that "You can't say it that way any more." You can't say it that way any more because, as Wallace Stevens had already discovered in "The American Sublime," "the sublime comes down / To the spirit itself, / The spirit and space, / The empty spirit, / In vacant space." The reinvention of the sublime on modern American ground requires an acceptance of emptiness, of a radical loss of presence. In Stevens's words, "One grows used to the weather, / The landscape and that"; and whether poets stand in the teeming wilderness or the teeming city, they must confront an ineluctable American vacancy.

The terms of the American sublime are in some respects more extreme than earlier notions of the sublime. Immanence and the withdrawal of immanence are experienced with an unbridled intensity: Whitman's vision of plenitude, his "chant of dilation," and Dickinson's confrontation with emptiness, her "Zero at the bone," inaugurate the American enterprise in poetry but also prescribe its experiential limits.

At the same time, Whitman and Dickinson insist that an American poetry be an ongoing, open-ended project shaped precisely to the contours of a life as lived: those highs and lows which constitute the sublime, those encounters of "The empty spirit / in vacant space," must be part of a continuous written enactment which is itself generative of plenitude and emptiness.

Sublime enactments of plenitude and emptiness within an ongoing, generative writing process: this rethinking of the lyric impulse in American terms is a crucial aspect of both Duncan's and Bronk's inheritance. Their responses to this inheritance, different as they may be, are informed by the continual possibility that, on the one hand, reality can flood the poem with meaning, so that its linguistic wealth pours beyond its borders; and that, on the other hand, reality can evacuate the poem of meaning, so that it becomes a sort of husk, with its language a mere shell around a hollow core. The poem that knows all, knowing itself as all; or the poem that knows nothing, knowing itself as nothing: how does one write poetry when faced with such extreme possibilities? This is a crisis indeed, one which Duncan and Bronk face very differently: Duncan through his passages across intuited orders of being, Bronk through his interrogations of rationality and belief.

Duncan, of course, turns to Whitman, "to be in the throes of a poetry in which the poet seeks to keep alive as a generative possibility a force and intent hidden in the very beginning of things, long before the beginning of the poem." The notion of a poetry prior to the utterance of the poem, of a hidden, generative force in the beginnings of all things, already contains within it this poetry of extreme fullness and emptiness. Consider the revelation in Whitman's brief poem "A Clear Midnight":

This is thy hour O Soul, thy free flight into the wordless,
Away from books, away from art, the day erased, the lesson done,
Thee fully forth emerging, silent, gazing, pondering the themes
        thou lovest best,
Night, sleep, death and the stars.

After the fullness of the day and its studies, a fullness of words and of activity, comes the silence of the generative void: "Night, sleep, death and the stars." For Duncan, such knowledge of the void is hermetic knowledge, as seen in one of his "Four Pictures of the Real Universe," called "The Closet":

> And does not the spirit attend secretly
> the music that is hidden away from me,
> chords that hold the stars in their courses,
> outfoldings of sound from the seed of first light?
> Were it not for the orders of music hidden
> we should be claimd by the preponderant void.

The preponderance of the void cannot be known through reason, but only through magic, as revealed to the poet-adept by his secret spirit attendant. This is *closeted* knowledge.

Like Whitman, Duncan recognizes the power of the silent void, but also celebrates the music of being, which cannot be perceived apart from that knowledge. The void dialectically generates Whitman's grand ensemble, or what Duncan names the grand collage: day and night, sound and silence, activity and contemplation, the void and the created universe are generative contraries for Whitman and Duncan, as they are for Blake and Yeats. From the void, magically, comes the universal orders of music which, although hidden from the poet, can be apprehended and enacted in the field of the poem, as in the close of Duncan's sequence called "Apprehensions":

> the orders of the sentence in reading;
> the orders of what is seen in passing. There was the swarming
> earth;
> the orders of commanding images;
> the orders of passionate fictions and themes of the poet in writing;
> the orders of the dead and the unborn that swarm in the flood of a
> man embracing his companion;
> the orders of the Lord of Love.

In his essay on *Roots and Branches*, Burton Hatlen defines Duncan's magic as "a systematic procedure for drawing together opposing forces, with the goal of healing and renewing both the self and the world." Imbued with the ancient knowledge "that the boundary of self and world is fluid," Duncan's poems do not usually present hermetic ideas but "are themselves magical acts that seek to unite opposites and thereby redeem the world." Thus, what the poem *knows* of the magical doctrine of opposites, of the preponderant void and the universal orders of being, informs what the poem *does* as it seeks to restore a fallen creation.

Now consider the following, which seems as far from a theurgic incantation as can be imagined:

No, it isn't a rational world but we say it is.
There is terror and the steep fall to chaos and the want.
We comfort ourselves: there *is* something, we say;
you have to make it, yes, but all right,
what else is the point? Study it, then, and work.
The mind is the mind; it shines its light in the dark.
Say *light* and the world is and it is the world.
Take care for it, take thought, take shelter there.

And it gives us away, it gives itself away:
the reasonable refuge world is the unreasonable.
To this madness or that is where we go.

Or stay. The horror here! Whether the world be rational
or the wild world be all
there is. No place for us. No place to go.

Bronk's poem "Nowhere" is surely born of knowledge of the void, "terror and the steep fall to chaos and the want." But against that knowledge are no countervailing assurances of order and harmony, no spirit-guarantors of apprehensible meaning. Instead, there is only human reason, an instrument which, if it knows anything, knows its inadequacy in an irrational world. Because it knows itself to be reasonable, the mind insists that the world is likewise orderly, that the dark can be illuminated through study and work. But that work—especially rational acts of language — soon gives way, as the seemingly rational world "gives us away, it gives itself away: / the reasonable refuge world is the unreasonable." Because every statement the mind can make about the world may be negated, because the mind can discover no ground of positive knowledge, the result of its study is madness, horror. The indeterminacy of knowledge in the face of the unknowable world turns what appears to be a "reasonable refuge" into "nowhere."

Bronk's thoroughgoing scepticism, so much at odds with Duncan's buoyant confidence, does not preclude the possibility of order, but it is not an eternal order open to poetic apprehension. Rather, for Bronk, order of any sort is always temporary, makeshift, "a world and not the world." The rational mind strains to create forms which ground us, house us, for they are our only bulwarks against the chaos, the existential emptiness which the mind knows reality to be. But in Bronk's work—and I see no sign of this in Duncan's—what becomes progressively more powerful and more frightening is not knowledge of the void, but intuition of an order which possesses us yet remains completely beyond us, indifferent to human life. Paradoxically, there are moments in Bronk's work when, through a process of negative transcendence, this awareness leads to an ecstatic state as moving as any found in Duncan's. The recognition of an infinitely remote and unknowable order becomes the ground for the negative sublime. "Objects are nothing," cries the poet in "The Annihilation of Matter"; "There is only the light, the light!"

One of the many poems in which Bronk examines the mind's relation to this impenetrable or unreachable order is "Ergo Non Sum. Est." The title, of course, plays off the Cartesian "Cogito ergo sum." For Bronk, "Cogito ergo non sum. Est": an "est" which simply cannot be spoken or thought:

> He said thinking assured his being; and was the same
> as he had been, which is to say not
> nothing exactly, — something is and we
> are part of it, but not by taking thought.

And yet, in a sense so: consciousness
is what comes through in thinking—what works.
That is, we don't make anything
but we become aware of being and it isn't ours.

And yet, in a sense so: something aware
of itself and we are nothing if not that.
That self: not only the instrument
of awareness but the self it is made aware of.

Thinking doesn't tell us what to say.
Awareness listens, tries, can't say.

This poem not only embodies one of Bronk's most common themes, but one of his most common procedures as well. From one assertion to the next, Bronk's poems usually appear in the guise of logical arguments, proposing, expounding, reiterating, and contradicting themselves. Yet as Ruth Grogan observes in her groundbreaking essay on Bronk's use of colloquial speech, "His language is often . . . the stuff of ordinary conversation among relaxed friends. And yet this disarming linguistic comfortableness is at the service of or simultaneous with an extreme rationalistic skepticism. It has the effect of expressing in homely terms the pathos of finding oneself, whatever that "One" or 'self' is, in an inconceivably vast, incomprehensible, and un-homelike universe, where all human constructs and relationships are only self-deceiving efforts to feel at home."

Thus, in "Ergo Non Sum. Est.," the process of reasoning—or, more precisely, talking about the process of reasoning—is both discovery and demonstration of reason's problematic worth in the human quest for self-understanding. The reasoning self is "not only the instrument / of awareness but the self it is made aware of"; nevertheless, "we become aware of being and it isn't our own." The "he," the figure of Descartes with which the poem begins, and the "we," the poem's speaker and the interlocutor of whom he is always aware, nearly disappear into the "est," the "it is" of an order which thinking or awareness "can't say."

Yet in the act of speaking, the "we" of this poem maintain a sense of their own being, despite what they learn of the overpowering "it." As Grogan points out, "the *saying* seems to exceed or contradict the *said* of the poems." In other words, what the poem does calls what the poem knows into question.

At the risk of being somewhat reductive, I can now state what might be called the polar difference between Duncan's and Bronk's understanding of language: it is the difference between language as magical or theurgic spell and language as rational or reasonable talk. In Duncan's case, the poem as magic spell is intended to perform an act of what the Jewish kabbalists call *tikkun olam,* restoration of the universe, a reunification of the orders of being. In Bronk's case, the poem as rational speech is intended to investigate the boundaries of mental life, to discover, if I may draw on three of Bronk's titles, "what form the world has," "the duplicities of sense," and how, finally, "the mind's limitations are its freedom." Yet as different as these two sensibilities are, both Duncan's and Bronk's poems repeatedly, obsessively thematize their own nature, their being as acts of language. We see this in Duncan's "Everything Speaks to Me" and Bronk's "Instead":

> Everything speaks to me! In faith
>   my sight is sound. I draw from out
>   the resounding mountain side
> the gist of majesty. It is at once
>   a presentation out of space
> awakening a spiritual enormity, and still,
>   the sounding of a tone
> apart from any commitment to some scale.

>   The sea
> comes in on rolling suds
>   of an insistent meaning, pounds
> the sands relentlessly, demanding
>   a hearing. I overhear
> tides of myself all night in it.

And in the sounds
that lips and tongue
and tunings of the vocal chords
within the chamber of the mouth and throat
   can send upon the air,

I answer. It is my evocation
      of the sound I'd have
return to me. My world in speech
answers some ultimate need I know,

aroused, pours forth upon the sands
      again and again
lines written for the audience of the sea.
               *   *   *
It is easy to see now that anything
I ever said was nothing: the slow words
seeming to particularize, delineate,
make real and touchable, —what were these?

Well, once a naturalness, accepting that,
of course, it was to see, to move and love.
I was. The world was. I spoke of it,
spoke to it, responded, sensed or made its shape.

It is unspeakable, that which exists.
All I ever said was spoken of what
is not, by one who is not. We do not speak
of that. Oh, we say. Make speeches, love.
And it is in place of what we would say,
what will not ever be spoken, cannot: is.

Apparently, the discourses of magic and of rational scepticism eventually turn back on themselves, address the conditions of their own making, the infinite possibility (in Duncan's case) or the impossibility (in

Bronk's) of their being. In both instances, linguistic self-consciousness becomes the engine driving the poem.

For Duncan, the poem is a response: in the act of utterance, it acknowledges and joins a language of creation which is forever articulating itself. The language of creation resonates within and is answered by the poet, a performance which brings speaker and listener closer to universal harmony. Duncan is an Adamic poet, a namer of the world, and an Orphic poet. According to Gerald Bruns in *Modern Poetry and the Idea of Language*, the Orphic poet's "sphere of activity is governed by a mythical or ideal unity of word and being, and whose power extends therefore beyond the formation of a work toward the creation of the world." Conjoined, world and poem are, as Duncan would have it, "a presentation out of space / awakening a spiritual enormity."

For Bronk, on the other hand, the poem is an observation, a *speculative* act of verbal decreation that begins in a casual remark and ends in stoic pathos. No longer able to accept an Adamic or Orphic role, Bronk transforms the lyric into a gesture of self-denial. It is self-denying in that it denies its own meaningfulness as utterance, in that it denies the speaking subject upon which it depends for its very existence, and in that it denies the world as ground of self and speech. But the poem cannot accept what one would assume is its inevitable alternative, that of silence. "Make speeches, love," says the insouciant poet. For speech, including the speech which constitutes the poem's being, stands "in the place of what we would say" if we could somehow speak for the "unspeakable," "that which exists," the "is" which is uttered at the poem's close.

Bronk's and Duncan's differing attitudes toward language, and hence toward the existential status of the poem, affect poetic form—the form not only of individual pieces, but of the entire body of each poet's work, how poem fits against poem in the continuum of writing. Matters of determinate and indeterminate form, of openness and closure, and of the beginnings and endings of poems come into play here, though these matters are inevitably implicated in the epistemological and existential questions about the lyric which I've already raised. As these issues join in our tracking of Duncan and Bronk, we approach the far border of poetry in our time.

Critics of Duncan's work especially tend to concentrate on these matters, and this is appropriate, since Duncan first came to the attention of the general audience for poetry as an exponent of open form, of "the new American poetry." Here are three quotations from Duncan s seminal essay "Toward an Open Universe":

> Central to and defining the poetics I am trying to suggest here is the conviction that the order man may contrive or impose upon the things about him or upon his own language is trivial beside the divine order or natural order he may discover in them.
>
> *   *   *
>
> In writing I do not organize words but follow my consciousness of—but it is also a desire that goes towards — orders in the play of forms and meanings toward poetic form.
>
> *   *   *
>
> Our engagement with knowing, with craft and lore, our demand for truth is not to reach a conclusion but to keep our exposure to what we do not know, to confront our wish and our need beyond habit and capability, beyond what we can take for granted, at the borderline, the light finger-tip or thought-tip where impulse and novelty spring.

These passages, and many more like them strewn throughout his extraordinary prose, indicate to what extent the discovery of form, or form as a process of discovery, is central to Duncan's poetic. The shape taken by an individual poem is discovered by the poet in accordance with a greater external order, an order toward which the poet *must* move but also *desires* to move, owing to an internal "desire for truth." What we know of "craft and lore" paradoxically impels us into what we do not know, those occult orders of form which Duncan so often invokes. What is revealed as the poem comes into being is part of what Duncan calls the *grand collage,* which, as Michael André Bernstein explains in his essay on Duncan and the idea of poetic influence, "is a process that represents itself primarily as a quest; more than anything else, it enacts the different paths a search for knowledge may follow."

The overall shape of Duncan's *grand collage* is worth our consideration, for it can help us focus our often imprecise understanding of "open form," which for Duncan is closely related to his magical view of language. What Duncan calls the "Form of Forms" accounts for the apparent heterogeneity of his poetic field. Poem to poem, Duncan can move from a whimsical ballad to a free translation of Dante or Baudelaire, to the symbolist prose of *The Structure of Rime,* to the indeterminate weave of *Passages,* to the sublime declarations of "This Place Rumord To Have Been Sodom" or "My Mother Would Be A Falconress." This is not mere eclecticism: the magical notion of corresponding universal orders to which Duncan subscribes includes the various orders of language as they both enter and produce the field of the poem.

But despite every poem's participation in the "Form of Forms," every poem also maintains its autonomy, with its frequently dramatic opening and its closing flourish. In his book on the forms of Postmodern poetry, Joseph Conte says of Duncan's *Passages* that "the closure of the individual poems is chiefly an assertion of molecular independence, not an insistence on thematic resolution. No section is reliant on or consequent to any other, and thus a linear-sequential reading of *Passages* is not permissible; each poem is independent of its predecessor, and so cannot be episodic. ... Although autonomous, each section continues to be conceived as a member of every other section, contextually interrelated."

I would expand this analysis to encompass the whole of Duncan's work. The relative autonomy or self-containment of individual poems, in the context of an unbounded totality, indicates that for Duncan, form is lawful. Each poem obeys an imperative to universal order by finding its sense of order, its unique laws of structure, in itself. The care lavished upon even the smallest units of composition, "the tone leading of the vowels," as Pound instructed the young Duncan to observe, reflects both an objectivist dedication to verbal precision and a kabbalistic faith in the magical power of every letter of the text, a power that literally holds the world together. "The secret world of the godhead," says Gershom Scholem, "is a world of language, a world of divine names that unfold in accordance with a law of their own. The elements of the divine language appear as the letters of the Holy Scriptures. Letters and names are not only conventional means of communication. They are far more. Each one represents a concentration of energy and expresses a wealth of meaning which cannot be translated, or not fully at least, into human language." One kabbalistic tradition holds that in the Messianic Age, we shall be able to read both the letters of the Torah and the white spaces which surround them. Another states that when the Messiah comes, God will reassemble the Torah's letters so that a Scripture of supreme truth will appear— the grandest of *grand collages*. From Duncan's syncretic perspective, all of language constitutes a kind of potential Scripture, a Book which, through the instrument of the poet, the Ineffable is always composing.

The verbal and metaphysical extravagance of Duncan's *grand collage* is answered by Bronk's mordant scepticism. At the ends of his most harrowing poems, the silence of the void is palpable; indeed, it is the counterpoint to every word which the poet writes. Bronk's rhetoric can be grand and elevated; it can be colloquial, even folksy; but regardless of its register, it comes into being as a protest and a consolation in the face of our ignorance, our worldlessness, and our ineluctable finitude. What Bronk calls "reality," "life," or "the world," that entity or condition of being which stands apart from us and which we can never know, creates, paradoxically, the possibility of a poetry that may be born out of any given instant of a life. In other words, because ultimately we know nothing of the world, all that we experience of the world may bring forth the poem. The autonomous status of each poem, its insistent singularity of utterance, is balanced by the momentary status it shares with all its fellows. In an interview with the poet, Henry Weinfield speaks of Bronk's sense of "dailiness": "[W]ith Bill, any *thing* in his life can go into his poetry. I don't know of anything that you do, any of your activities, that in some way can't find their way into your poetry, transformed in terms of a poetic conception." To which Bronk replies, "I lie in wait for it."

The irony of that metaphor—poet as hunter, subject matter as prey — is that over the course of Bronk's career, the relationship has been quite the reverse. A more apt metaphor is found in "It Comes to This":

I have been spouse to my art for all my years,
coming to it naked or in country clothes. The craft
it dressed me in was the art's, not mine.
Though I say without shame that I did bring my body food,
I know it wasn't enough, that, beyond the food,
the art fed me, kept me alive: in its keep.
Whatever of value I have, I have from it
and I have been all my life a kept man
who is ignorant now of the value of anything,
of what it is and of how or why it should be.

Thus, it is not merely that "Life keeps me alive," as Bronk says in the poem "Life Supports"; rather, the art keeps him alive, in order that the poems may be produced through him. As in Duncan's case, we return to the poet as instrument, but for Bronk, the instrument "is ignorant now of the value of anything."

To what extent the poet really is an instrument, to what extent an agent, is a longstanding debate which we cannot enter on this occasion. Let us set the figure of the poet aside and think instead of poetry, especially lyric poetry, as an instrument, an instrument to probe our knowledge of being. Yet unlike other instruments, it is also a good in itself, what Duncan calls, in "Poetry, A Natural Thing," "a spiritual urgency at the dark ladders leaping," what Bronk names, in "The Nature of Musical Form," "fairness stating only itself." That the statement of fairness can be felt as a spiritual urgency, that we yearn for form both for itself and for what it tells us about ourselves, is a point on the far border of poetry to which Duncan's and Bronk's work surely leads us. And so we have arrived, to discover that the poetry we want is a poetry that fulfills our urgencies even as it fulfills itself.

What are those urgencies? What desires do we inherit from such figures as Duncan and Bronk that set the tasks of poets who follow them? From the poetry of recent years that I have found the most compelling, and from my own urgencies as I write, I think I can discern a number of answers.

The dailiness to which American poetry has long been dedicated still has power over us, though after Duncan's magical households and Bronk's speculative abstractions, dailiness means something very different to us than to the earlier modernists. We are not content to celebrate it, to stoically endure it, to criticize it in the name of some higher truth, or even to remake it through imaginative sovereignty. Perhaps we have returned more to the spirit of Whitman and Dickinson, for the quotidian must end in revelation, or if it does not, it must prove to be a revelation in itself. By revelation I mean, awkwardly, some sense of "beyondness," some sense of a further horizon which inheres in our notion of the sublime.

So in addition to and as a complement of a poetry of dailiness, we want a poetry of the inspired mind, a poetry that may follow the contours of life as lived but is always leaping beyond that as well. It may be a restorative poetry, as with Duncan, or a speculative poetry, as with Bronk, though in the greatest work of both, these two functions cannot be separated. "The dark at the center of being," says Bronk in "The Verges of Happinesses," "is seldom seen / until the verges are lightened" and I think that Duncan, however differently he lights those verges, would agree.

For some today, lighting the verges around the center of being requires a poetry of linguistic investigation, revealing language to be the ground—the groundless ground—of our dailiness and of our most rarefied reaches beyond. As Michael Palmer says at the end of his poem "Voice and Address,"

You would like to live somewhere

but this is not permitted
You may not even think of it
lest the thinking appear as words

and the words as things
arriving in competing waves
from the ruin of that place

In these lines, a fascination with the magic of language competes with the most severe linguistic scepticism. Certainly we have had, and will continue to have, a significant poetry of this sort, and I have tried to show how Duncan and Bronk, especially in their heightened linguistic self-consciousness, anticipate this development in some respects.

This leads me to wonder, given poetry's increasingly threatened status today, if the horizon or beyond toward which the writing of our lives ultimately directs us is simply form, the poem itself. "The Nature of Musical Form," which is surely one of Bronk's greatest lyrics, opens with just this observation:

> It is hard to believe of the world that there should be
> music in it: these certainties against
> the all-uncertain, this ordered fairness beneath
> the tonelessness, the confusion of random noise.

Yet there is, as Duncan insists, a music

ascending to where the beat breaks
   into an all-but-unbearable whirling crown
of feet dancing, and now he sings or it is
   the light singing, the voice
shaking, in the throes of the coming melody,
   resonances of meaning exceeding what we
understand, words freed from their origins,
   obedient to tongues (sparks) (burning)
speech-flames outreaching the heart's measure.

Even in our less ecstatic moments, I hope we would agree.

SOME REFLECTIONS
ON POETIC INSPIRATION

I

In reading the literary criticism of T. S. Eliot, one often feels that the figure of the poet in the act of writing is always in a mentally unbalanced or emotionally disturbed state. Hence the famous distinction, in "Tradition and the Individual Talent," between "the man who suffers and the mind which creates," as if the suffering poet suddenly enters a momentary condition of mental health in which the poem comes into being. And in the Conclusion to *The Use of Poetry and the Use of Criticism,* Eliot speaks of a poem coming to one in "ill-health" as if it were automatic writing, which "may succeed in standing the examination of a more normal state of mind." The poetry which results from these circumstances probably has been "incubating" in the writer for some time; contrary to popular belief, it is not "a present from a friendly or impertinent demon." Thus Eliot psychologizes moments of inspiration, as most modernists would, and in this respect he may be usefully compared to the daemonic line, which in our century extends from Yeats, with his voices who have come to give him metaphors for poetry to Jack Spicer, with his spooks and Martians.

But in the Conclusion, Eliot then makes a judgment of those moments, and in doing so, redefines what we conventionally understand to be inspiration, even when we think in psychological as opposed to daemonic terms: "To me it seems that at these moments, which are characterised by the sudden lifting of the burden of anxiety and fear which presses upon our daily lives so steadily that we are unaware of it, what happens is something *negative:* that is to say, not 'inspiration' as we commonly think of it, but the breaking down of

126

strong habitual barriers—which tend to re-form very quickly. Some obstruction is momentarily whisked away. The accompanying feeling is less like what we know as positive pleasure, than a sudden relief from an intolerable burden." Later, he speaks of poetry helping us, therapeutically as it were, because we become "a little more aware of the deeper, unnamed feelings which form the substratum of our being, to which we rarely penetrate; for our lives are mostly a constant evasion of ourselves, and an evasion of the visible and sensible world." Poetry affects a change in us similar to the self—realization at some crucial point in the course of psychoanalysis: where id was, there ego shall be. In that we live in a state of evasion, unable to face the psychic truth about ourselves, poetry comes to us as a breaking of our defense mechanisms, our "strong habitual barriers." We are at risk, but we are no longer deluded—at least temporarily. Such is the composition of the poem for the poet, and presumably, such is the recapitulation of the poem for the reader.

Inspiration then, according to this model, is a psychological event coincident with an act of writing, in which preexisting elements (effects coincident with words and verbal patterns) come together unexpectedly. To be sure, this act of synthesis, of articulation, yields something new; but the creation of the new is simultaneously a comprehensible alignment of all that has come before. Changing, shifting, and variously exerting psychic and verbal pressures, the stuff of accumulated experience suddenly becomes energized, "takes on a life of its own" as inspired poets might say. The resulting poem orders and clarifies what was previously psychically and linguistically inchoate. Regardless of how obscure the work might be—to readers or even to poets themselves—it is literally of a higher order of consciousness than that which has produced it. Hence Eliot's sense of the poem's arrival as a relief from an existential burden as well as a therapeutic encounter with what previously could not be admitted or faced.

An ironic complement to this view of inspiration is to be found in the psychoanalytic tradition itself. In "Psychoanalysis and Education: Teaching Terminable and Interminable," Soshana Felman says of literature that it *"knows it knows, but does not know the meaning of its knowledge."* For Felman, literary knowledge is unique in that it is "knowledge that is not in mastery of itself"—and it is the same sort of knowledge that is to be gained from dreams and from the free association of patients in psychotherapy. This non-authoritative knowledge, which is the foundation of psychoanalysis, of teaching, and of literary interpretation, has its origin in the ancients' understanding of inspiration. Felman cites Socrates, who, in the *Apology*, discovers that the poets cannot provide the interpretations of their own works which he seeks: "Then I knew that *not by wisdom do poets write poetry, but by a sort of genius or inspiration;* they are like diviners or soothsayers who also *say many fine things, but do not understand the meaning of them.*" Traditionally, the daemonic notion of inspiration has been the only way to account for the psychological (and hermeneutic) phenomenon of non-authoritative wisdom, of writing which claims authority only in spite of itself, since it does not come into being through a fully conscious mental state.

Freud himself acknowledges this unique quality of the poet's power at the beginning of "The Relation of the Poet to Day-Dreaming." What makes the poet able, Freud asks, "to carry us with him in such a way and to arouse emotions in us of which we thought ourselves perhaps not even capable? Our interest in the problem is only stimulated by the circumstance that if we ask poets themselves they give us no explanation of the matter, or at least no satisfactory explanation." For Freud, the poet's sensibility or psychic disposition is such that he can perform astonishing acts of emotional invocation; but what he calls forth in his readers, the emotional changes that he works upon them through his art, cannot be understood as the result of his authority on any except the aesthetic level. While Freud fully acknowledges the poet's masterful technique, it is an intuitive formal power and not the power of conscious knowledge, of knowing that he knows. Technique, "the essential *ars poetica*," is the poet's "innermost secret," through which his otherwise unpalatable fantasies, his day-dreams, come to us as the most pleasurable works of art. The poet's transformation of his fantasies, achieved through his unfathomable mastery of technique, creates aesthetic pleasure, which is actually a "fore-pleasure" because it puts readers "into a position in which we can enjoy our own daydreams without reproach or shame."

By now we are at a great remove from Eliot's view of inspiration as sudden relief. If anything, the Freudian view of inspiration is that of artful elaboration and rearrangement, a building up of form rather than a breaking down of barriers. The poet's unconscious knowledge and secret technique produce a form through which he and his readers can pleasurably—and publicly—indulge in a mental activity that has become, since our departure from childhood, rather unseemly, a strictly private affair. Enlarging and transforming psychic material which we would ordinarily guard or even repress, the poet's inspired art is simultaneously an art of revelation and disguise. In the moment of composition, Freud argues, "Some actual experience which made a strong impression on the writer had stirred up a memory of an earlier experience, generally belonging to childhood, which then arouses a wish that finds a fulfillment in the work in question, and in which elements of the recent event and the old memory should be discernible." The compounding of old memory, recent event, and wish fulfillment (past, present, and future), a process which cannot be a matter of consciousness, results in a form. The poet brings together apparently unrelated experiences from disparate points in time and makes one moment, one utterance, one work of them. To be sure, we know that something new has come into existence: we take in the aesthetic pleasure it has to offer and are dimly aware of what goes into the making of such pleasure. This is not, as Eliot would have it, a penetration or breaking through to truth; rather it is an evasion of and fabrication out of truth. But only through such fabrication can we know that there is truth to know.

II

What follows are some reflections of a more personal nature, based on my own experiences of poetic inspiration. These move between the models I have adduced from Eliot and from Freud. Despite what I consider my rational inclination, I wish I could accept the daemonic notion of inspiration in its purest version: poetry is a gift (or an imposition) from the beyond; we take dictation from a voice which suddenly begins to speak; and any labor expended upon the poem is a matter of following the contours of that utterance as closely as is humanly possible. But though I may proceed at times as if this is the case, I cannot accept it—not merely because of inclination, but because my praxis indicates that a more psychological orientation is necessary. If writing poetry is listening to an incoming voice (Spicer's poet-as-radio), then I know all too well that the voice is mine. It could be the voice of a hidden self, and at the moments when I'm pleased with the work, it could be the voice of my best self. But when I write, I usually feel the stirring of too much inchoate inner material to flatter myself into believing in any sort of visitation.

Thus I would like instead to believe that poetry comes to us—or rather, that we come to poetry—through Eliot's process of penetration. Given the unavoidable personal stake in the work, the great investment of ego that goes into writing poetry, it is gratifying to think that the poem, among other achievements, is the achievement of an insight which previously had been kept from us or which we had kept from ourselves. Writing the poem becomes a struggle for honesty—not necessarily in terms of raw autobiographical confession, but in accord with what the Objectivists call "sincerity." The poet's devotion to the ideal of truth, perceived in the circumstance of a moment, is borne out in what we feel to be the poem's inevitable language. World and self suddenly are in sync, and the poem attests to a direct confrontation, free of the usual defenses, at the truest level of being.

But just as I cannot be satisfied with the idea of poetry as dictation, neither am I content with the view of poetry as a breakthrough in psychic being. Too often in the course of writing a poem, I watch myself swerve away from some utterance that possibly would lead to some greater truth about myself or my world. Even in the course of a few lines, I find myself elaborating an otherwise intolerably severe statement, so that only the ghost of its meaning—a meaning which it seems I am unwilling to fathom—remains in the precincts of the text. Those are the moments when I find my own words the most chilling, the moments when I am most tempted to believe in the daemon, who, however terrible a taskmaster, would ease the burden of the self. Then I know that our poems are our evasions; that we lavish upon them all our verbal skills because there are other words we can scarcely bear to pronounce. Freud is kind to poets, for he honors those skills, but he is still more stern with us than we can usually afford to be with ourselves. His view of the poem as a work of wish-fulfillment, of fantasy compounded out of lingering, reactivated traces of memory, darkens the triumph of our invention. If our poems are pearls, they are formed around endlessly irritating grains of sand.

Ironically, it was Yeats, for all his otherworldly experiences, who came to understand this more intimately than any other modern poet. Each time I read "The Circus Animals' Desertion," I shudder anew at the fortitude required in naming "the foul rag-and-bone shop of the heart." What was previously an unacknowledged process of making becomes, at the end of a long career, the conscious subject of the poem. The result is a masterful illusion: the poem, especially its last lines, appears to consist of the raw stuff of mental life, and yet we are also aware of what a refined and technically sophisticated verbal production it is. Longing to be done with artifice, to reach down into the substratum of being, results in a heightened power of artifice. So perhaps the greatest lyric poems simultaneously break down and build up. They treat the details of one's life like precious truths won in hard psychic struggle and like so many elements to be arranged into patterns of fantasy and desire.

That poetic inspiration partakes of both discovery and fabrication, of both revelation and artifice, is not, of course, a matter that disturbs me (or, I imagine, most other poets) when the work is going well—that is, when the material is there, tractable and full of promise. There is something about the poem coming easily that obviates any speculation regarding its origin. This feeling is akin to the occasional sense of redundancy, not downright irrelevance, experienced by the critic interpreting a poem or the teacher explicating it in class. What, after all, can one say about the poem that it cannot say about itself? This frustrating, chastening awareness of tautology (which, incidentally, poses itself against Felman's notion of literature as knowledge which does not know its own meaning) extends from the most sophisticated hermeneutical gestures, through the first reading encounters, and back to the poet meeting the work as it comes into being. The poem that instantly represses the conditions of its making, leaving only a lingering sense of sudden revelation or of long labor, will be the same poem that successfully eludes even the most canny attempts at paraphrase. The poem's declaration of autonomy, which all critics, regardless of their orientation, must oppose, is an interdiction against any conjecture as to its beginnings. Only insecure poets, who doubt the sufficiency of their utterance, engage in such conjecture. But what poet is free of such doubts as these?

III

In 1911, three years after "The Relation of the Poet to Day-Dreaming," Freud returned to the figure of the artist in "Formulations On the Two Principles of Mental Functioning," the essay in which he clearly distinguishes between the pleasure principle and the reality principle. According to Freud, "*Art* brings about a reconciliation between the two principles in a peculiar way. An artist is originally a man who turns away from reality because he cannot come to terms with the renunciation of instinctual satisfaction which it at first demands, and who allows his erotic and ambitious wishes full play in the life of phantasy. He finds his way back to reality, however, from this world of phantasy by making use of special gifts to mould his phantasies into truths of a new kind which are valued by men as precious reflections of reality. . . . But he can only achieve this because other men feel the same dissatisfaction as he does with the renunciation demanded by reality, and because the dissatisfaction, which results from the replacement of the pleasure principle by the reality principle, is itself a part of reality."

This passage confirms what Freud asserts in his essay on daydreams, and insists even more strongly that it is the desire for gratification and the frustration with reality which unites artist and audience. We are eager to take what the poet has offer because we intuit that fantasies of pleasure—and the thwarting of such fantasies—are at the heart of the poet's metamorphic work. Poetry comes into being through a subtle dialectic of the pleasure principle and the reality principle: the poet's work involves a simultaneous indulgence in fantasy and renunciation of fantasy, a dissatisfaction with reality that constitutes reality.

This dialectic, apparently, is both theme and procedure of the work; it is as it has come to be, and we respond most deeply to the hidden narrative of its making.

If this were the complete psychological scenario regarding inspiration, then the poet's lot would be relatively secure and happy. Poetry could then be regarded as a nimble movement, part intuition, part craft, between gratification and denial, an austere but ultimately rewarding art which in turn represented a humane and mature world view. On the constitutive plane of language, the poet would appear as the most skillful of negotiators, the artist who, more than any other, could masterfully shape the stuff of mental life, however it shifted with the sad vicissitudes of external reality.

But this is not the whole story, at least within the psychoanalytic tradition. In *Freud and Philosophy,* Paul Ricoeur comments on the view of art in "The Two Principles of Mental Functioning": "if art initiates the reconciliation between the pleasure and the reality principles, it does so mainly on the basis of the pleasure principle. In spite of his great sympathy for the arts, Freud has none for what might be described as an esthetic world view. Just as he distinguishes esthetic seduction from religious illusion, so too he lets it be understood that the esthetic—or, to be more exact, the esthetic world view—goes only halfway toward the awesome education to necessity required by the harshness of life and the knowledge of death, an education impeded by our incorrigible narcissism and by our thirst for childhood consolation." I would venture to guess that there are times in the lives of all poets when the aesthetic world view proves insufficient, when the making of poetry, which is a perpetual self-education ("the vale of Soul-making," as Keats would have it), fails to compensate for "the renunciation demanded by reality." Those are the occasions when the wounds to our narcissism pain us most sharply, when it is not the muse who breaks down strong habitual barriers, but Ananke herself, Freud's strong goddess of fate. What results at such moments is never poetry, though poetry may follow later, reminding us, after the crisis passes, of what it can and cannot do.

But if the return of poetry must be inevitably a return, at least in part, to "childhood consolation," then it also signifies the resumption of our education out of childhood, in which poetry always plays a part. Thus Ricoeur observes thatif art cannot take the place of wisdom, it does lead to it in its own way. The symbolic resolution of conflicts through art, the transfer of desires and hatreds to the plane of play, day-dreams, and poetry, borders on resignation; prior to wisdom, while waiting for wisdom, the symbolic mode proper to the work of art enables us to endure the harshness of life, and, suspended between illusion and reality, helps us to love our fate. When I think of what I want for my own poetry, I can think of no more apt description than that of a work suspended between illusion and reality which helps me and my readers love our fate. But in saying this, I wonder if I do not betray my belief in poetry as the embodiment of desire, the force opposed to limitation and necessity, which propels language to the horizon of the imagination. I can only trust that this is not the case: it is the fate of poetry to oppose fate, to seek, in the space between illusion and reality, a love that is for itself, that builds its world, however much it recognizes its kinship with death.

POETRY AND EMOTION

"ONLY EMOTION ENDURES" declares Ezra Pound at the end of his seminal essay "A Retrospect" (1918). The figure most often associated with the transformations which American poetry undergoes at the beginning of the twentieth century, Pound sees emotion as fundamental to poetic value, but is at the same time reluctant to specify the means through which emotion endures. Those verbal qualities which express the poet's emotion and which in turn move the reader of the poem are elusive and difficult to define; as Pound says in the same essay, "if we still feel the same emotions as those which launched the thousand ships, it is quite certain that we come on these feelings differently, through different nuances, by different intellectual gradations." Thus changes in poetic style and the development of new techniques and devices are, in effect, intended to maintain poetry's emotional force. For Pound, nearly the only identifiable linguistic quality consistently found in poetry of great emotional impact is clarity. As he says in "How to Read" (1929), "One 'moves' the reader only by clarity. In depicting the motions of the 'human heart' the durability of the writing depends on the exactitude. It is the thing that is true and stays true that keeps fresh for the new reader." Emotion in itself cannot make for good poetry, for emotion in itself, however sincerely felt by the individual, has yet to become a "thing that is true," that is, a verbal form or object. Poets, therefore, are not merely emotional individuals who set their feelings down in verse of whatever style. To quote Pound once again, from "The Serious Artist" (1913), "I suppose that what, in the long run, makes the poet is a sort of persistence of the emotional nature, and joined with this, a peculiar sort of control." In composing poetry, the writer's emotional sensibility must in itself be controlled, and the language through which emotion is expressed must be controlled as well. The poet struggles to bring language to feelings, and to charge language with feeling. Pound's criticism demonstrates that in considering the expression of emotion in poetry, and hence the role of emotion in poetic composition, romantic exuberance is always in conflict with classical restraint.

To the popular mind, romantic exuberance takes precedence in this debate, for the popular conception of poetry is that it is fundamentally self-expression, an outpouring of feelings that may be decorated by metaphor and cast (though not necessarily) into meter and rhyme. Poetry is thus regarded as the art of the emotions par excellence, a notion that takes on definitive authority with the advent of Romanticism in the late-eighteenth and early-nineteenth centuries. But even as central a statement of the Romantic aesthetic as William Wordsworth's Preface to his *Lyrical Ballads* (1800) indicates the degree of importance which the Romantic poets attached to matters of intellectual control and verbal precision. To be sure, for Wordsworth the emotional capacities of the poet are of the utmost significance. Yet in his most famous formulation of the relation of poetry to emotion, we find that thought is just as important as feeling: "For all good poetry is the spontaneous overflow of powerful feelings: and though this be true, poems to which any value can be attached were never produced on any variety of subjects but by a man who, being possessed of more than usual organic sensibility, has also thought long and deeply." Throughout the Preface, Wordsworth associates poetry with pleasure; providing "immediate pleasure" is the one necessity of poetic composition, which he otherwise regards as an experience of the greatest freedom. (It is worth noting that the final section of Wallace Stevens's masterpiece, "Notes toward a Supreme Fiction" [1942], is likewise entitled *It Must Give Pleasure*.) But the process of composition, through which pleasure is produced, is equally a matter of thought, a subtle interaction of heart and mind. Wordsworth's description of this process, however later poets have modified or argued against it, still provides us the clearest understanding of emotion's role in poetry as both inspiration and content, and of the importance of conscious thought as well: "[Poetry] takes its origin from emotion recollected in tranquillity: the emotion is contemplated till, by a species of reaction, the tranquillity gradually disappears, and an emotion, kindred to that which was before the subject of contemplation, is gradually produced, and does itself actually exist in the mind. In this mood successful composition generally begins, and in a mood similar to this it is carried on; but the emotion, of whatever kind, and in whatever degree, from various causes, is qualified by various pleasures, so that in describing any passions whatsoever, which are voluntarily described, the mind will, upon the whole, be in a state of enjoyment."

Wordsworth's understanding of poetic form, especially meter, which prior to the advent of free verse was understood to distinguish poetry from prose, is directly related to his emphasis on pleasure, and on the excitement of the emotions that poetry produces. Because "[t]he end of poetry is to produce excitement in co-existence with an over-balance of pleasure," then "the co-presence of something regular, something to which the mind has been accustomed in various moods and in a less excited state, cannot but have great efficacy in tempering and restraining the passion by an intertexture of ordinary feeling, and of feeling not strictly and necessarily with the passion." Wordsworth's concern with the regularity of meter (which in this respect is analogous to Pound's emphasis on the poet's sense of "control") is yet another indication that even among poets for whom the expression of emotion is paramount, the deliberate artifice, the crafted poem, must make its "co-presence" felt by writer and reader.

The power of poetic form to universalize the individual's emotional life, making the experience of private or inner feeling accessible to poetry's general audience, has been a subject of frequent critical speculation. In "Tradition and the Individual Talent," the essay which may be said to inaugurate modern literary criticism, Pound's colleague T. S. Eliot argues strongly for what he calls the "Impersonal theory of poetry." As an advocate of classical restraint and an explicit opponent of Wordsworth's position, Eliot regards the origin of poetry as "neither emotion, nor recollection, nor without distortion of meaning, tranquility. It is a concentration, and a new thing resulting from the concentration, of a very great number of experiences which to the practical and active person would not seem to be experiences at all." Eliot stresses linguistic concentration rather than meditative emotion: when we are moved by a particular passage in a poem, we are in contact with feelings that are not necessarily derived from the emotional life or private experience of the poet; rather, it is the concentrated power of language that moves us to an intensity and complexity of feeling that merely lived events usually cannot provide. This is why, in Eliot's view, "[h]onest criticism and sensitive appreciation is directed not upon the poet but upon the poetry"; furthermore, "very few know when there is an expression of *significant* emotion, emotion which has its life in the poem and not in the history of the poet."

Eliot regards the mind of the poet in the act of composition as a catalyst. The poet is possessed of a highly refined sensibility, but unlike Wordsworth, for whom the poet must be "a man pleased with his own passions and volitions, and who rejoices more than other men in the spirit of life that is in him," Eliot's poet "has, not a 'personality' to express, but a particular medium, which is only a medium and not a personality, in which impressions and experiences combine in peculiar and unexpected ways. Impressions and experiences which are important to the man may take no place in the poetry, and those which become important in the poetry may play quite a negligible part in the man, the personality." The individual poet's capacity for feeling is by no means irrelevant in Eliot's theory, but that individual's talent as a "medium" is developed less through lived experience than through exposure to the great works of literature which precede the new work. Emotion endures in and through tradition, what Eliot calls "the main current" or (allowing for his limited cultural perspective) "the mind of Europe." This mind is "much more important that [the poet's] own private mind," for it is in the historical continuity of significant literary forms that the individual poet finds the means to universalize private experience. Personal feelings in themselves are therefore regarded with a good deal of suspicion. Hence Eliot's notorious declaration that "[p]oetry is not a turning loose of emotion, but an escape from emotion; it is not the expression of personality, but an escape from personality. But, of course, only those who have personality and emotions know what it means to want to escape from these things."

Although many readers find Eliot's snobbery objectionable, the notion of the impersonal poet who serves as a catalyst or medium for the refinement of emotional experience is not uncommon, and is held by writers of rather different temperament and ideological orientation. John Keats, Wordsworth's younger contemporary, argues in one of his letters (to Benjamin Bailey, 22 Nov. 1817) that "Men of Genius are great as certain ethereal Chemicals operating on the Mass of neutral intellect—[but] they have not any individuality, any determined Character." Deeply influenced by Wordsworth's view that the poet is an individual attuned to the emotional nuances of life, Keats nevertheless departs from his mentor because Wordsworth privileges what Keats calls "the egotistical sublime." Keats readily acknowledges the importance of personal feeling to poetic composition, but rather than emphasize the gradual emotional growth of the autobiographical self (Wordsworth's major poem, The Prelude, is subtitled "Growth of a Poet's Mind"), he regards the "poetical Character" as emotionally indeterminate, "every thing and nothing": "It has no character—it enjoys light and shade; it lives in gusto, be it foul or fair, high or low, rich or poor, mean or elevated" (letter to Richard Woodhouse, 27 Oct. 1818). Keats's understanding of the poetic self is centered upon emotional exuberance or intensity rather than specific emotional content; he declares in the same letter that as an individual, "A Poet is the most unpoetical of any thing in existence; because he has no Identity—he is continually in for—and filling some other Body."

At the same time, however, the poet must be continually conscious of the emotional tenor of shifting experience, of life as it is lived. "I am certain of nothing but of the holiness of the Heart's affections and the truth of the imagination" Keats declares in the letter to Bailey cited above. The instability of the poetic identity is directly related to the imagination, through which the poet's emotional responses to the world are tested and given form. Keats names such responsiveness "Negative Capability, that is when man is capable of being in uncertainties, Mysteries, doubts, without any irritable reaching after fact & reason" (letter to George and Thomas Keats, 21 Dec. 1817), and naturally credits Shakespeare with a great measure of this power. Composed without preconception, a poem charged with emotion is the result of the poet's openness to experience. The feelings expressed in such a work, and the feelings elicited in the reader, are not those of private individuals, but pertain to a universal state of being which the poem makes accessible. Keats calls the world "The value of Soul-making" (letter to George and Georgiana Keats, 21 April 1819), for the emotional experience that is latent in the world gradually forms and educates the human heart.

Poetry is, in effect, the record of that process; hence its importance for any theory of the emotions. Poets have been traditionally regarded as individuals who are particularly sensitive to the nuances of the emotional life. Yet as we have seen, they also possess the linguistic means to articulate these nuances and even more importantly, make them into beautiful forms. The appreciation of these images lead the readers to an empathetic state of mind, a state in which emotions are mostly deeply felt and understood. And yet a poem is a poem, a verbal pattern, and not the emotions it evokes. In his *Anatomy of Criticism* (1957), Northrop Frye argues that "Poetic images do not state or point to anything, but, by pointing to each other, they suggest or evoke the mood that informs the poem. That is, they express or articulate the mood. The emotion is not chaotic or inarticulate: it merely would have remained so if it had not turned into a poem, and when it does so, it *is* the poem, not something else still behind it." Feelings are relatively ephemeral, and over the course of a lifetime, even the strongest currents of love and joy, anger and sorrow tend to fade after the intensity of the events that first produced them recede into the past. But if such feelings should inspire a poem, they will come to life again each time the poem is read.

Up until now, I have not distinguished among particular genres of verse, but I assume that the lyric (as opposed to epic or dramatic poetry) is that type of poem most closely associated with emotional experience, or the representation of emotion in personal or individual terms. By lyric I mean a relatively short poem in which the sensual and musical qualities of language are heightened in order to present a subjective, emotionally charged moment, an interior event with lasting resonance. Emotion, obviously, plays a great part in the development of narrative structure and characterization in epic and dramatic poetry, and any reader can recall scenes of overpowering pathos in the greatest works in these genres, such as the encounter with Paolo and Francesca in Dante's *Inferno* or the meeting of the blinded Gloucester and Edgar in Shakespeare's *King Lear*. It is no accident that, as we have seen, Keats invokes Shakespeare when presenting his idea of negative capability, and he is thinking of Shakespeare the dramatist, who enters more fully into the emotional being of invented personalities than any other writer before or since.

In "Everything and Nothing," his extraordinary parable of Shakespeare's life, Jorge Luis Borges speaks of an uncanny emptiness in the poet which impels him to create the multitude of passionate personalities found in his plays. At the time of his death, he finds himself in the presence of God and cries "I who have been so many men in vain want to be one and myself." God replies that "Neither am I anyone; I have dreamt the world as you dreamt your work, my Shakespeare, and among the forms in my dream are you, who like myself are many and no one." Borges's insight into the godlike quality of Shakespeare's negative capability proceeds to influence Harold Bloom's account of Shakespeare's canonical centrality. In *The Western Canon*, Bloom asserts that one of Shakespeare's greatest contributions—not only to literature, but to the human self-image—lies in the way his major characters "become free artists of themselves [the phrase is Hegel's], which means they are free to write themselves, to will changes in the self. Overhearing their own speeches and pondering those expressions, they change and go on to contemplate an otherness in the self, or the possibility of such otherness." In other words, the volatile situations in which these characters find themselves produce emotional states which, through their poetic articulation, lead them to self-knowledge and to actions that further transform their inner lives. In Shakespeare's dramatic verse, emotions are not simply felt; they become the objects of self-reflection and thus powerful motivations in the shaping of an individual's destiny.

However permanently and powerfully our understanding—indeed, if what Bloom says is true, our very awareness—of the emotions is transformed through Shakespeare's drama, it remains the case that since the Romantic period, the lyric is commonly regarded as the poetic form of emotional expression. Appropriately, Bloom credits

Wordsworth with inventing the modern poem, in which the "subject is the subject herself or himself, whether manifested as a presence or as an absence." Just as poetry is popularly regarded as self-expression, the lyric is popularly regarded as the poetic form through which that subjectivity is expressed. The utterance with which we are confronted in a lyric presupposes a single speaker, and the use of the pronoun "I" in such a poem leads us to identify the intensity of this utterance with the emotional condition of the poet, the individual who has actually written the poem. The immediacy of this association is crucial to the artistic effect of the poem: when Emily Dickinson declares "I felt a Funeral, in my Brain / And Mourners to and fro" (#280), we assume that the deathly feelings of psychic weight and oppression reported in the text, if not strictly autobiographical, are nevertheless derived from the poet's intimate knowledge of these feelings. The reader enters into an unspoken contract with the poet; we assume that the emotions conveyed by the poem are real, are true. As Frye says in the *Anatomy of Criticism*, "[t]he radical of presentation in the lyric is the hypothetical form of what in religion is called the 'I-Thou' relationship," which is fundamentally a relationship of reciprocity and trust. In the twentieth century, when the stability and unity of the subject have been radically interrogated by various trends in such disciplines as psychology and philosophy, as well as by literature itself, lyric poetry is still a matter of language measured by emotional truth, even when the poet must, in all responsibility, register the most severe doubts about the process. "As soon as / I speak, I / speaks" declares Robert Creeley in "The Pattern." The doubleness of the poet's personhood as expressed by the shift from first- to third-person may deliver an existential shock to the reader (perhaps no greater than Dickinson's funeral image), but although the self that feels is called into question, the truth of that feeling remains.

In his *Anatomy*, Frye calls the lyric "preeminently the utterance that is overheard. The lyric poet normally pretends to be talking to himself or to someone else: a spirit of nature, a Muse (note the distinction from *epos*, where the Muse speaks *through* the poet), a personal friend, a lover, a god, a personified abstraction, or a natural object." The idea that the lyric is an overheard utterance, that the poet's back is turned to the reader, leads to the question of the relationship between lyric poetry and society. Are poets merely pretending to turn their backs, or is that gesture which initiates the lyric utterance a genuine rejection of the social in favor of the personal? How does the privacy, the intimacy implied by the emotional expressiveness of the lyric utterance move from the level of "I-Thou" relationship to that of a generalized "we"? Frye's answer is that each lyric poem expresses an archetypal pattern of recurrence, and the emotions it embodies are subordinated under the general force of desire, or "wish-thinking." For Frye, lyric expression is metonymic of the human process of civilization, "the process of making a total human form out of nature." The emotional power of a poem is the power of desire, "the energy that leads human society to develop its own form. Desire in this sense is the social aspect of . . . emotion, an impulse toward expression which would have remained amorphous if the poem had not liberated it by providing the form of its expression." Frye, who began his career as an archetypal critic studying the visionary poetry of William Blake, is profoundly Romantic in this formulation. In the poem, what the individual feels is what human society feels. When the poem achieves the heights of emotional expression, we meet "a vision, not of the personal greatness of the poet, but of something impersonal and far greater: the vision of a decisive act of spiritual freedom, the vision of the recreation of man."

Other critics, however, find the relation between the apparently personal stance of the lyric poet and the social function of poetry to be more problematic. The passionate expressivity of a great lyric may represent Frye's "decisive act of spiritual freedom," but why should we conclude that this freedom is anything more than a momentary instance of an individual's rhetorical power? "At the lyrical moment," observes Georg Lukács, wrestling with the same issue in his *Theory of the Novel* (1916), "the purest interiority of the soul, set apart from duration without choice, lifted above the obscurely-determined multiplicity of things, solidifies into substance." For Lukács, the strength and the weakness of the lyric lies in the momentary quality of its emotional intensity, for "only in lyric poetry do these direct, sudden flashes of the substance become like lost original manuscripts suddenly made legible; only in lyric poetry is the subject, the vehicle of such experiences, transformed into the sole carrier of meaning, the only true reality." The experience of pure interiority is hardly consistent: sudden and individualized, an emotional state expressed in a lyric utterance impresses us as "the only true reality" for a moment only, and cannot be sustained. Yet paradoxically, the momentary feeling of a lyric poem can resonate with a reader for a lifetime. How then do we account for what may be termed the poem's "social power"?

In "Lyric Poetry and Society" (1957), T. W. Adorno observes that "what we mean by lyric . . . has within it, in its 'purest' form, the quality of a break or rupture. The subjective being that makes itself heard in lyric poetry is one which defines and expresses itself as something opposed to the collective and the realm of objectivity." The intimate feeling-states of lyric poetry come into being on the far side of a divide between the individual poet and the social collective. In Adorno's analysis, that which bridges the gap is not the feelings expressed in the poem, however commonly felt they may be, but its language: "The most sublime lyric works, therefore, are those in which the subject, without a trace of his material being, intones in language until the voice of language itself is heard. The *subject's* forgetting himself, his abandoning himself to language as if devoting himself completely to an object—this and the direct intimacy and spontaneity of his *expression* are the same. Thus language begets and joins both poetry and society in their innermost natures." In Adorno's formulation, the poet's devotion to language causes the private self to dissolve into the greater social being, but with no loss of the "intimacy and spontaneity" we ordinarily associate with the expressive power of the passionate individual.

Language, then, is always the determinant of the poem's emotional truth. The radical simplicity of the greatest lyric verse, and the overriding sense of inevitability we feel moving from line to line in such poetry, are the results of the poet's giving of the self to language, which enlarges the self and opens out its emotional condition. A linguistic community comes into being, as in William Bronk's poem "The Tell":

I want to tell my friends how beautiful
the world is. Not but what they know
it is terrible too—they know as well as I;
but nevertheless, I want to tell my friends.

Because they are. And this is what they are;
and because it is and this is what it is.
You are my friend. The world is beautiful.
Dear friend, you are. I want to tell you so.

The poet's desire to "tell" of his feelings is so strong and pure that only the most direct and simple language can match the dignity—and urgency—of that desire. Against all that is terrible in the world, we are given the poet's friendship and vision of beauty. This is how poetry sustains our emotional lives.